IBIZA

A MEDITERRANEAN LIFESTYLE

IBIZA
A MEDITERRANEAN LIFESTYLE

FRITZI MARCHIONESS OF NORTHAMPTON

Text by

LLUÍS DOMÈNECH

Photographs by

CONRAD WHITE

KÖNEMANN

Original edition © Lunwerg Editores, Barcelona, 1999
Text © Lluís Domènech
Photos © Conrad White

Original title: Ibiza. Isla de los Tesoros

Copyright © 1999 for the English edition
Könemann Verlagsgesellschaft mbH
Bonner Str. 126, D- 50968 Cologne

Translation from Spanish: Lucilla Watson
Editing and typesetting: Book Creation Services Ltd.
Project coordinator: Tami Rex for Book Creations Ltd.
Production: Ursula Schümer
Printing and binding: Neue Stalling, Oldenburg

Printed in Germany
ISBN 3-8290-2226-3

10 9 8 7 6 5 4 3 2

Contents

Introduction

The task of writing on the Ibizan houses that form the subject of this book could only have been carried out by identifying the common threads that connect these buildings. These common threads are the dreams, in the widest sense of the word, that the houses express, and these dreams inevitably form an integral part of the text that follows.

They are the starting point for the impetus that led the owners of these houses to build or renovate them. Each of these dreams is very real; some of them are very beautiful, others capture the faint echo of a glimpsed paradise, reflected in a mirror that ironically reveals other accidental urban realities, which sometimes conspire to frustrate and from which one wants to flee.

The inhabitants of these houses, men and women from all over the world, have sought isolation on an island within an island; they seek to defend their privacy and, although they do not explicitly say as much, they try to be true to themselves, a difficult aim to which humankind has aspired from antiquity. Many of these people have severed the umbilical cord that connected them to urban life; others have willingly adopted a schizophrenic lifestyle, returning to the city for business reasons.

It would be vacuous and repetitive to ask why Ibiza has for so long been a kind of miniature magnet that draws different people to it, not only on account of its Mediterranean beauty but also originating from something deep within the earth itself, something that bestows a special identity, connected to an ideal existence, on those who have become deeply rooted in Ibizan soil. That there are so many people whose lives have been transformed by the power of the island must be more than historical coincidence. They range from legendary Phoenician sailors and Arab poets, significantly called "El Sabina" and "El Ibiza" (examples that even in the 1960s the canon-historian Macabich explained), to more recent arrivals of people and the work of such architects as Erwin Brönner, José Luís Sert, German Rodríguez Arias, or travelers like Albert Camus and Walter Benjamin, who visited only once but whose sensibilities were marked forever.

It is possible that, as the Ibizan philosopher Toni Mari has said, "alienation from any center of civilization preserved the island's dreamlike integrity, recreating a past that feels as if it is absolutely the present and projecting a future that becomes lost in the past." This is a dream that has in the past half-century been gradually truncated and that the owners of the houses illustrated in this book wish to preserve. They are lovers of nature, not only of the land, which is obvious in our Nordic visitors, but of the sea and the countryside, of the boats and the fish, the flowers, the olive trees, the figs and the pines, of sunrise and sunset, and of the cold still months of January.

They are aware that the island is severely overrun by mass tourism and they seek to preserve that small part of it that belongs to them, although they know very well that they are too individualistic to organize themselves into more ecologically caring and efficient groups.

But for them, the Ibizan dream is also the dream of freedom whose various aspects – leisure, love, contemplation, creativity, friendship, happiness – are enjoyed sometimes with admirable peacefulness, at others with irrepressible enthusiasm. In general, the island appears generously to accommodate the desires of the different generations that have succeeded one another in an inexorable rhythm, a rhythm very beautifully marked by the ebb and flow of the sea.

The different buildings described in this book therefore comprise a doubly artificial landscape. In a physical context they are exceptions in a landscape that precariously survives. In a social context they are small havens that are generally isolated from urban Ibizans, who together with their political leaders have done little collectively to preserve the environment. With their positively tolerant attitude, this special group of foreigners has been exemplary. Recently, ecologists have gathered considerable strength as a group force and their precepts underpin the trail that the Belgian architect Philippe Rotthier blazed in 1984 with the publication of the ground-breaking book *Le Palais Paysan* ('The Rustic Palace').

The selection of houses that feature in the pages that follow do not truly constitute an island within an island; rather they form an archipelago, multifaceted and diverse, comprising different elements, and whose large number is surprising on such a small island. One of the fundamental aims of this book is to celebrate this multiplicity, the multiplicity of many different dreams that Ibiza has planted in people's minds.

For this reason, in the text that accompanies each house the description of the architecture is interwoven with a description of the personality of its owner, the latter being essential to the understanding of the former.

In the illustration and description of the buildings that follow, the aim is in no way to express a particular point of view or pass any narrow esthetic value judgment. Within the limits necessarily imposed by a selection, the purpose of this book is to illustrate a diversity of architectural entities that express the reality of those Ibizan dreams, dreams that D. H. Lawrence summed up when he said: "Whoever wants the world to be perfect should take the precaution of having no real likes or dislikes. Universal goodwill is all that one can allow oneself."

Lluís Domènech

Photo: Raymar

Acknowledgments

Lunwerg Editors would like to thank

ALEX JAUMANDREU, ANNA MARQUARD, ANTONIO FACHINI, ANTONIUS LOOMAN,

BEATE WEDEKIND, DECORUM IBIZA, ELENA CALDERÓN, FOTO LAB RITU IBIZA, GÖSTA FRIEDRICH GASSMANN,

HOTEL OCEAN DRIVE, HRH PRINCE ERNST OF HANOVER, IBIZA FILM, SALOMON ENGELSMAN, IRMA KUYPER,

JAIME ROIG, JOHAN STENSEN, JÖRG MARQUARD, JUAN SEIX, LOUISA COMPTON, LEONIQUE WHITE,

MARGREET HERTEL, PHILIPPE ROTTHIER, PRISCILLA NEWMAN, ROBERT TWEEBEEKE AND JOHN BROEKMAN,

ROLPH BLAKSTAD, ROSER AMADO, SANDY IVAN PRATT, SOL D'EN SERRA IBIZA,

THE PHILOSOPHER TONI MARI, THE WATCH GALLERY, THE ROCK BAND THE WELL OFFS,

THE OWNERS OF THE ALL THE HOUSES THAT FEATURE IN THIS BOOK, TONI AND SUZAN TORRES, "Zoë and Chloé"

Ibizan panorama

La Peña (Photo: Viñets)

The Treasures of the Island

Lluís Domènech

Ibiza possesses many treasures. The first is the island itself, with its landscape of blue sea and reddish earth, rough rocks and sunny orchards where oranges and apricots grow alongside mint and jasmine. The second is the people that have inhabited the island throughout history: peasants, shepherds, and sailors who equated the world with the island and with themselves, and who, in the words of Antonio Colinas, "found in that place the inner self that is born of resignation, self-sufficiency, effort, and acceptance, and of contemplation."

The third treasure, which sums up and links the two others, is the architecture, the Ibizan house, or *casa payesa*, an enclosed microcosm, the nucleus of existence, the focal point of life, of work, and of pleasure, a place of truth. Albert Camus, a writer who reconciled the sense of life with the inner world of ideas, was in Ibiza in 1935. He wrote: "Ibiza: a bay; Sa Peña, a fortress. Santa Eulalia, the beach, the party. The cafés in the port. Stone walls and windmills of the countryside."

This close integration of landscape and life was described by Rafael Alberti, who also lived for a time in Ibiza during the outbreak of the Spanish Civil War:

Come again, gnarled
ever-magical wonder of old olive trees.
Let your roots embrace me anew, burying
me in the tombs that show their loneliness
    to the sun.
I want to touch you, hallowed, indestructible
    fig trees,
weighed down by fruit but not by weariness.
Let me sleep peacefully in the still, close darkness
of your cool bedchamber.

In a much earlier age, Al-Makkari, an Ibizan-Arabic geographer, had recorded this colorful description of the treasures of the island: "Ibiza supplies a large area of Africa with wool and salt. The island is densely populated and its inhabitants are very industrious: they grow all manner of cereals and fruits, but the wool-producing animals do not multiply; there are goats, the meat of which is used for food. Grapes, almonds, and figs are the produce that the natives grow and export to the nearby island of Mallorca. In Ibiza there are no olives: they are unknown to the islanders, who import olive oil from Andalucía. As there is much woodland in Ibiza, the major industry is charcoal-burning, the charcoal being shipped to Barcelona and other Mediterranean ports."

Thereafter, in the 15th century, when the Atlantic sea routes had been discovered, the Mediterranean sank into profound isolation, and Ibiza fell into a period of decadence in which its inhabitants had to find their identity in their land and defend it. The Ibizan poet Marià Villangómez wrote:

> *Those men fought.*
> *They heeded warning*
> *and it was also with blood that they sowed*
> *that land.*
> *Hardened hands grasped tools and weapons.*
> *They defended life, crops, their meager possessions.*
> *Peasants and soldiers, the task was one:*
> *to drive the plow into the earth or the knife into the*
> *enemy.*
> *Those centuries brought*
> *armed raids and hostile drought.*
> *From the sea came storms*
> *and enemy ships like angry clouds.*

This balanced relationship between the island, its people, and the city persisted well into the 20th century. Albert Camus bade farewell to the island dazzled by the beauty of this aspect of Ibiza.

"In Ibiza every day I went to sit in the cafés that line the port. At about 5pm, youngsters passed by in double file along the quay. Proposals of marriage were made

there, all of life was there. You cannot stop thinking that there is a certain grandeur in starting off in life like this, in front of everybody. Then I would sit, overwhelmed by a day of sun, full of white churches and gray walls, arid land and olive trees. I would drink a sickly sweet *horchata*, contemplating the outline of the hills before me; they sloped gently down to the sea. The evening took on a greenish light. In the hills a last gust of wind turned the sails of a windmill. And, by some natural miracle, everyone lowered their voices, so that there was nothing left but the sky and a murmur of words rising up, though they sounded as if they came from a great a distance. This brief instant in the dusk was filled with something fleeting and melancholy, that touched not only one man but a whole town. For my part, I wanted to love as you can want to cry. It seemed to me that, from then on, every hour of sleep would be an hour stolen from life."

And María Teresa León, the poet who accompanied Alberti on his Ibizan sojourn, exclaimed: "... it is impossible to have had fonder memories of life than we have of that brief time ... Ibiza... my God ... never have I been so happy ... If only we could all be together on the most beautiful island in the world." Alberti, a native of Cadiz, couched his vision of the island in more poetic terms:

Windmill, where is your millstone
taking me?
You are no windmill.
I had a windmill
with black and white sails.
Island of blue pines.
Island of fig trees.
Ibiza stretches out blue.
I was a prisoner
on a mountain of pines.
My life was a hut
made out of a parasol
and sea breezes.

Toni Mari, a philosopher and a native of Ibiza, focuses directly on this matchless power of the Ibizan countryside, this vital emanation that comes from nature itself:

And I saw the silence
And we sensed the silence.
And we saw how in the silence
Those omens grew
How the bird grew
How the trees and the houses grew.
How the city and the dream grew.
How everything grew.

Ibiza is therefore a transmission of life. From the germination from the earth, from the heat of the sun or the brightness of the moon spring forces that transmit themselves to people:

It is the woods, the woods that are returning!
Those woods where love, turned inside out,
pricked itself on brambles

and was like a happy canyon, lit up
with little stars of the sweetest blood!
...those nights in which love burned
like the one god who inhabited the woods.

Everything was fire at that time. The beach
blazed around you. Seaweed, molluscs, and stones
were reduced to glistening glass
that the waves cast up against you.

Past is the blue-imbued siesta
that the wide island brought to us in sleep.
Venus, still slumbering, leads you
to the last mooring place of boats
and you sing of everything like a harbor
that loves sails and masts.

Alberti captured magnificently this telluric impulse that Tanit, Venus, or any of the contemporary goddesses beneficially impart to the island.

Cilette Ofaire, a Swiss painter and writer who has made Ibiza her home, arrived on the island in 1936 aboard her yacht *L'Isme* and despite the Spanish Civil War stayed and settled permanently in Ibiza. She sums up her experience thus:

Then, a voice said:
Quit living.
Another said:
Quit working.
Outside, a blackbird was singing.

From the earth and from people buildings emerged. Over the centuries, there

evolved in the rural Ibizan house a refined relationship between its function, its construction, and its form. At the beginning of the 20th century, the crisis that middle-class art, as well as the architecture of the period, was undergoing in a time of general uncertainty led some people to realize that vernacular Ibizan building styles could serve as a model for a totally new architecture. José Luís Sert describes his discovery, through Erwin Brönner, who had arrived in Ibiza in 1933:

"In 1933, a young German architect contacted our group GATCPAC in Barcelona. He was writing to us from the island of Ibiza, which at that time was virtually unknown, enclosing a collection of photographs and plans that were a revelation to our organization. The photographs showed Ibizan farmhouses and one or two churches that had a unique simplicity and beauty. The plans, accurate and neat, had been drawn with the utmost care. Brönner, who was familiar with our magazine, *A.C.*, which was then in its infancy, demonstrated to us that we were all thinking along the same lines.

We had found a soul mate, who like us was searching for new directions, new horizons, and who showed us this vernacular architecture that transcended style or period."

The land and its architecture meld into an organic whole, as Sert, whose wish it is to be buried on Ibizan soil, explains:

"Rural houses are built with dry stone walls that are usually painted white. It is as if these houses had miles and miles of stone roots that make up one of the elements of the island's landscape, because there is not only an architecture of the house but also an architecture of the landscape."

The more analytical Walter Benjamin, writing to Gretel Adorno in 1932, discovers to his fascination this timeless architecture, the fruit of Ibizan wisdom: "The inhabitants isolate themselves from each other by a skillful use of space and walls nearly 3 feet thick that admit no sound (nor any heat)."

So strong is the ancestral relationship between the Ibizan rural house and its surroundings that it has given rise to mythical interpretations.

"The traditional architect gives much thought to the position of the plot of land and to the forces of nature: the sun, the wind, and water courses. He tries to determine where to sink the foundations. He takes note of the vegetation, the burrows made by animals, the natural rock formations.

"Perhaps he also tries to detect the power lines of the earth's crust, the earth's electromagnetic fields, their points of convergence and their lines of rupture. To do this, he can observe which areas are chosen by animals known for their sensitivity to these forces: the preferred

pasture of certain domesticated animals, the burrows or the nests of wild animals. Wasn't this the way that the spot where Carthage was to be built was chosen by Dido, the queen, who had noticed how her cattle lay down in a favorite spot?"

Philippe Rotthier, an architect who is active today and who has designed one of the converted houses that are featured in this book, sums up the phenomenon thus:

"The typical Ibizan house consists of a limited number of solutions that are repeated over time and improved as the result of the experience of everyday living in an ecosystem; they are adapted and perfected but above all respected. It is the perfect symbiosis between the mode of production and resources.

The Ibizan *casa payesa*, as a type, has a set of standard characteristics. The forms and techniques used are the result of repeated usage (a stereotype) of the same material, of the same methods, and the same spatial units, linked to social and family needs, the origins of which go back to time immemorial. The perpetual repetition of the

same processes spring from one fount of technical knowledge, but above all from a liturgy, which traditional societies hold preeminent in all religious matters."

The quotations that appear above are taken from: *Viatge a las Balers Menors*, by Baltasar Porcel; *Rafael Alberti en Ibiza*, by Antonio Colinas; *Monografía Erwin Brönner; Revista D'A. Ibiza; La Nave de Piedra*, by Atonio Colinas and Toni Pomar; *Architecturas de Philippe Rotthier*, AAM; *Le Palais Paysan*, by Philippe Rotthier.

Can Lluquí

The statue of King Gudea of Lagash, regarded as one of the most important objects in the Louvre, is a fascinating piece of sculpture; for all that it appears expressionless and inscrutable, it conveys a profound feeling of inner life. The king, the greatest of men in ancient Sumer, was a sage and a priest, the one who knew when to sow and when to harvest the crops, how to build houses and who to invoke so that men should act in harmony with a single cosmic force. Gudea holds in his hands a measuring instrument and issues rules on all manner of subjects from mathematics to moral codes and commercial matters, in one of the earliest human endeavors to live in harmony with nature.

Researchers have traced Ibizan culture, rural and insular in nature, to complex cultural traditions that from 5000 BC intermingled across a wide band centered on the 40th parallel. This was the civilization of the arid lands. Phoenician sailors were to establish this culture in Ibiza, and Rolph Blakstad, who has worked there for over 30 years, interprets this culture not as a fossilized phenomenon but as a living entity that is still alive today.

In the valley that gently slopes southward from Puig des Fornás, at an altitude of 145 feet, down to envelop the cluster of houses in Morna, it is hard not to think of King Gudea, and all that governed where to locate a house in the landscape, how to orientate it, plan it, and build it – a house geographically so far removed from the houses of Sumer, of the Atlas Mountains, of Ladakh, of the valleys in Yemen, yet so similar; measured words, the words of the Gudeas of this world, had a profound

effect on those who heard them. In the valley, forming a sort of triangle with two neighboring houses, is Can Lluquí, one of the purest examples of the rural Ibizan house. Restored and altered by the Belgian architect Philippe Rotthier, another great expert on Ibizan architecture, Can Lluquí is both conceptually strict and formally majestic.

Access to rural houses, which are south-facing and perch above the steepest part of a hillside, is almost always from the side. The carob

The frontal appearance of Can Lluquí expresses the strong mythical and ritual elements of the Ibizan house, while the organic development of its component parts (following page) serves the needs of practical everyday living.

trees, almond trees, and fig trees half conceal a white mass that, as it is approached, gradually reveals its full extent. Of the juxtaposed white cubes, only the rear portion corresponds to the house itself. The portion at the front represents the outline of the entrance courtyard and other outbuildings. Although they are not very large, these houses give the impression of being firmly and permanently rooted in the soil.

Above this first impression of the house, its frontal aspect appearing as a deeply rooted mass standing against a background of dark pines, floats the sound of music, the clear, energetic strains of a suite or partita by J. S. Bach. Typically, the house is oriented on a north-south axis, its northern side being set into the living rock so as to protect it from the wind, and descending in stages toward the south. However, it gradually becomes clear that the house also slopes slightly in a west-to-east direction; the kitchen is at a slightly higher level but is counterbalanced by the tower. Likewise the plain eastern wall, with its little central window, has its counterpoint in the chiaroscuro of the terrace above the kitchen. Bougainvillaea and wisteria offset the

harsh vibrancy of the whitewashed walls within which lies the *porxo*, a lobby that is invariably rectangular and invariably in the same place with regard to the orientation of the house. This is the nucleus of the Ibizan house, to which other rooms can be added according to need; most typically, these additions take the form of a pair of rooms located to the rear of the *porxo*.

Strains of Bach continue to weave a subtle tissue of sound. The room leads through to the dining room, on a slightly different floor level; this space is dominated at one end by a great chimney piece, and at the other by a narrow staircase whose upper landing emphasizes the height of the ceiling. At both ends of the room overhead lighting wells bring out a magical texture in the walls. These lighting wells were the idea of Philippe Rotthier; they cannot be called restoration, nor even imitative pastiche; they are, rather, in the genre of subtle conversion, the inspiration that comes to architects through silence, observation, or communion with the building, through listening to the wind or letting inspiration come from the sight of golden dust playing in a shaft of light.

Staircases and different floor levels are typical
of the Ibizan rural house.

The House in the Olive Trees

There are many different ways of going about fixing up an old Ibizan house, but these do not usually involve the use of a Geiger counter. The reason for this is not connected with any unwelcome nuclear arsenal that slumbers forgotten in the interior of the island but with something more subtle: the presence of electromagnetic fields, fault lines, and other curious founts of energy that appear to abound deep in the Ibizan subsoil. It is a matter of locating the "good waves," the positive energies. This search has been led by a couple who, living in the old house where they had lived for many years, wanted to extend it so as to add rooms for their wide circle of friends and relations and also build a new extension for their own bedroom.

The husband is an Italian architect who is of the generation that during the 1950s and 1960s saw in their own country the development of the best architecture in Europe. With his steely gray eyes, high forehead, and a voice with a hint of melancholy that betrays the fact that he is no stranger to disappointment, he is also one of those northern Italians who are closely related to central European stock. The wife is the more typically Italian of the pair; she is a sculptress in the style of a Naum Gabo or a Brancusi. For all that, she is obviously pragmatic in domestic affairs. She is also very interested in theories concerning electromagnetic fields. In Ibiza, she says, this type of radiation is very powerful and, accordingly, one must both avoid its ill-effects, caused by the radon gas that escapes from fractures in the earth, and take advantage of its beneficial powers, which can be tapped at certain points in these electromagnetic fields. The search for favorable magnetic fields has been the focus of her life over the last few years and she determined that the bedroom that her husband was planning to build, and preferably the bed itself, should be set exactly over the spot where these "good vibrations" were to be felt.

The lively discussions that took place between such a difficult client and the indulgent architect are not hard to imagine. As it turned out, the crucial point was located several dozen yards away from the spot on which stood the old Ibizan house in which they were living, and the architect had to devise a means of making a logical and harmonious connection between the old and the new. A passageway was the obvious solution, but he made of this feature an exquisite art gallery where the work of his grandfather is now displayed, a talented Italian painter whose canvases are stored in the house in Milan.

But this episode apart, the house is a fine example of the integration of vernacular and modern architecture. The problem stems from the fact that old Ibizan houses are closely linked to the landscape in a very particular way. They are well finished

in that their proportions, orientation, and the various floor levels were precisely adapted to the land on which they were built, but they are simultaneously unfinished in the sense that extensions could be added according to need, which in turn would result in a new well-finished house. The challenge facing the Italian architect was how to build a new, "separate" component, in a modern idiom and without the many affectations of the landscape gardener, the latter consideration being well justified given the nature of the terrain.

The house stands on a gentle slope, one of the few plots of land with mature olive trees that still exist in Ibiza. The sea breeze coming in from Els Cubells has bent them over toward the mountains, the Sierra de la Murtra, which shelters the area from the cold north winds.

The old house rambles in a series of stages down the south-facing incline. The various rooms now serve as areas for living, cooking, and sleeping, and also as work-spaces, the architect's studio being a well

The traditional and the contemporary blend harmoniously in the rooms of this house.

thought-out fusion of rural Ibizan architecture and the sober refinement of Milanese design.

The new wing was designed along more radical lines. The picture gallery that links the old house with the modern bedroom passes underground, being lit from above and by a cleverly excavated sunken courtyard. Turning to good advantage the unevenness of the terrain, the bedroom is also built partly underground; only the roof is visible, emerging like an *objet trouvé* between the olive trees. Beneath the largest of them, a contented couple continue with their amicable discussion, the sound of the woman's voice punctuated by gentle interjections from the man.

The underground passageway linking the art gallery and the bedroom.
Previous page: a *trull*, a traditional Ibizan olive press, becomes part of the furniture in the extension to the main part of the house.

The wide corridor linking the old house with the new wing, which houses the bedroom, was turned into an art gallery. The heated swimming pool, built partly underground, is like a grotto and opens to the exterior on one side.

Can Novell

"*Blau*" is a word that means "blue" in Catalan (or Ibizan) and also in German, and blue – the radiant azure of the Mediterranean environment – is a color that has been used by the German artist who lives in this house to express her ideas on the victory of the spirit over prejudice and intolerance.

This woman, with her husband, a businessman, and their two children, live in Can Novell. Although they entertain a few friends, they prefer to live a reclusive existence, guarding their privacy, an existence that is in complete contrast to the hectic lifestyle in Berlin to which they return several times a year. They came to the island in 1982 and in 1986 purchased this old house, which in fact consisted of two houses belonging to two Ibizan brothers. The duality of this building's roots has inevitably affected its structure; its heterogeneous character has been increased by new additions and by the construction of a studio for the painter.

The fact that the house should be seen in terms of the interplay of elements that go back to its dual origins is not unconnected to the strong, very different personalities of

the two owners. One is more focused on action and on the immediacy of the appeal of the Ibizan landscape; the other is more thoughtful and analytical, an approach that finds expression in her delicate and often ambiguous artistic output.

Every aspect of the interior decoration of the house illuminates this sometimes tumultuous combination of personalities. A multitude of different objects, shapes, colors, and styles reflect a powerful collector's mentality quite as much as thoughtful and meditative spiritual development. Lamps in Murano glass, something that is especially prized by the woman of the couple, sums up this ambivalent attitude. On the one hand she admires the technical skill that it represents and prizes it for its monetary value; on the other it is its almost melancholy beauty and the pale iridescence of its ever-changing colors that she loves.

It may be that this heterogeneity, set apart from the context of the house, has other causes: consciously

Previous pages: the counterpoint of the component parts that make up Can Novell, a feature common to all Mediterranean houses, is the result of adding to the building according to need and of continuity between the different elements.

or unconsciously, the couple carry memories of their previous lives in Berlin, England, Italy, and New York, and this comes out in their cosmopolitan tastes, in a multifarious juxtaposition of elements that seem to hark back to the expressionist tastes of someone who still remembers her early attachment to the German neo-fauvist movements.

Nevertheless, the clear, immutable, serene central reference point of all this is the Ibizan landscape, which can be admired from the countless terraces, doors, and windows of the house. In front the hills that surround Santa Eulalia stretch away; nothing spoils the view of row upon row of ocher and pink almond trees, carob trees, and fig trees; beyond distant clusters of pine trees appears the fine, continuous line between sea and sky.

The house has a highly complex ground-plan, given that the two existing buildings each had their own nucleus, each expanding independently from that nucleus with the addition of cubelike rooms and the one linked to the other by the juxtaposition of their outer rooms. The house that stood on the western

A kind of decorative collage, superimposed styles, the accumulation of objects from a previous life and complex creativity characterize Can Novell.

side formed a compact nucleus, while that on the eastern side expanded on a north-south axis, spreading out downward in a typical series of buildings that once housed the animals.

These farm buildings, closely clustered together, have been converted into guest-rooms. The original main room of the house on the western side, meanwhile, is now a spacious living room, decorated with an imaginative, baroque scheme in which the predominant color is red. A new wing with a large sitting room with painted ceiling and columns leading to the porch has

also been added to the eastern part of the complex.

Floors, windows, painted walls, furniture and objects join together in a frenetic, multicolored dance that leads us back to the imaginary world of the painter, to her soft, delicately executed brushtrokes that weave into a cosmic collage of fragments of the most ordinary daily reality. "Nothing about the figures that I paint, nothing about the faces or the bodies, seems permanent. What underlies it all is a style of painting that distorts facial features and at the same time forges a unity between figure and surface."

The expressive ideas of the mistress of the house can be seen in every corner of Can Novell.

The various outbuildings, resulting from the fusion of two old houses, lend themselves to some very original treatment. This is made possible only by the variety and scope offered by Ibizan architecture.

Can Pere Jaume

the upper story. The house was purchased by Grillo Demo in 1980. After a hectic period of traveling between his native Argentina and New York City, London, Paris, and Milan, this was to be his bolt-hole. Demo set about refurbishing the house, which expresses both his love and understanding of vernacular Ibizan architecture, as well as the irrepressible desire to furnish and decorate it creatively.

Demo is an artist who is not restricted to a single medium; his wide ambit embraces painting as well as design, both of which for him are marked by a strong sculptural sense. He began by applying his creative flair to the garden, filling it with typical Mediterranean plants, which he chose for their color, for their shape, and most particularly for their beguiling scent. All these plants – bougainvillaea, which in no time seemed to become part of the structure of the house; mimosa, which blossoms in February, when spring is still a long way off; roses and many varieties of jasmine – wrapped themselves around the house, became part of the fabric of

On a bend in the Santa Eulalia river, near where the little watercourse flows into the ocean at a spot marked for miles around by the rise of Puig de Misa, stands Can Pere Jaume, a modest old rural dwelling that once belonged to two brothers of that name. Like every watercourse in Ibiza, the river is bordered by clumps of reeds, which are used to build makeshift huts as well as to make the ubiquitous baskets. Against this backdrop of reed beds, on a gentle south-facing slope, stands a house whose distinguishing and most prominent feature is the triple arch of

the rough walls of the ancient enclosures, and invaded the porch. Demo's aim was to bring nature right to the doorstep of the house and to create an environment in which the distinction between indoors and outdoors was all but obliterated.

The porch and upper terrace, and other parts of the house that were obviously open to the great outdoors, were furnished as comfortably as any sitting room. By contrast, in the rooms within the house, nature could be experienced at first hand through the windows, or artificially by way of the murals, painted by Grillo Demo himself, on the theme of the sea or the countryside; in the kitchen, a spacious room that has been tiled in the traditional manner, Grillo has painted directly onto the tiles a *trompe l'oeil* of windows in which fish swim by; in the living room, murals expound on the arcadian theme of wheatsheaves.

From an early age, Grillo Demo felt the urge to capture visual impressions and give them various forms. His eye has caught an infinite

The Ibizan climate allows a close relationship, sometimes brought about in unexpected ways, between the interior of the house and the world out of doors.

Ibizan handicrafts and folk art are collected, prominently displayed and transformed by being given a new use or by the addition of other elements.

number of images that have presented themselves during the course of his itinerant life and these images fill numerous pages of his "travel notebooks", which he proudly shows as the repository of studies for what will eventually be finished works. To while away the hours that he has spent waiting in airports, he has explored physical form, including distortions of reality, dreamlike images, collages, false perspectives,

and so on. Not unexpectedly, considering his compulsive drive, the walls of his house are one great "travel notebook," in which the dreams of his wild fantasy are recorded, painted, and displayed. Against this background, Demo has arranged rugs, carpets, chaises-longues, tables and chairs, furnishings that make for physical comfort and a supremely welcoming atmosphere. And there are quantities of candles, reminiscent of Seville's churches in Holy Week, replete with romantic images of the grieving Virgin.

Demo's creativity as a designer has led him to design furniture for the David Gill gallery in London; these mushroom-like objects fill the old porch, the lobby of the house, the emblematic initial space that leads to the other rooms of the house. His study, on the mezzanine, is full of newspaper cuttings and issues of *Interview* – the magazine in which Demo has published some of his most arresting watercolors – which point to the close relationship that he still maintains with artistic circles in London and New York.

Leaving behind the sun, we go up to the gallery. Golden light flows in through the three slightly flattened

arches, with their archaic capitals, that frame the windows, and falls on the Moroccan carpet and the sofa upholstered in Mallorcan fabric. A few branches of wisteria scramble over the dark wooden roof beams. A mirror, a gilt Indian tray, and a silver Tibetan bowl reflect the rosy light.

The scent of the flowers in the garden and the aroma of candles is something that no photograph can convey.

Casa de los Angeles

About 30 years ago, and quite in keeping with the spirit of the times, Antonio Facchini, the son of an engineer from Udine, in Italy, fell in love with Ibiza and settled on the island. In 1978, putting his budding interest in antiques to practical use, together with Jörg Marquard, he established the Galería del Elefante, in Dalt Vila; for many years this was a landmark for visitors who climbed the steep slopes that led up to the cathedral. With Jörg, Antonio has restored and decorated a large number of houses for the colony of foreigners who live in Ibiza and, on account of his reputation and sound judgment, he has long been in unique demand among people who were looking for a "place in the sun" where they could build the house of their dreams. Antonio bought his present house in 1982 from an Ibizan who had had business connections with Cuba. Of his original estate, over 1000 acres in extent, he sold off a 675-acre plot of land attached to the house, which is set in the little valley that runs parallel to the road leading to Santa Gertrudis.

From the outside, the house has a curious appearance: it is a combination of an Italian villa and a colonial mansion, with elegant tiled eaves setting off the red plaster that outlines the white expanses of doors and windows. The building is typical of the kind of house that Ibizan families would return to live in, having left some time before to settle in towns and cities elsewhere.

The practice of selling off the great agricultural estates has not been so pronounced in Ibiza as it has been in Mallorca, because in Ibiza everything is done more discreetly and on a smaller scale. But from the 1920s, in the years following World War I, the trend has been unstoppable. Antonio Facchini, an authority on the subject, caustically explains how women who inherited the poorest land, from the point of

A dreamlike ambience of transparency, *trompe l'oeil* landscapes, and a heterogeneous mixture of styles.

view of agriculture – that is land nearest the ocean – were those who came out best when it came to selling it for development. Antonio explains all this with a sense of ironic resignation, which he applies to himself and to this house: this house, the Casa de los Angeles, is also reputed to have ghosts. One misty morning he saw a beautiful blonde girl in an elegant white dress with a red sash wandering in the garden.

She walked about for a while, floating in and out of the plants, and then she disappeared. The next day, still electrified by what he had seen, Antonio spotted a handsome white horse in the garden. This was just too much, and Antonio ran to tell his neighbor about his visions. "Oh, that one," he replied gravely, and went on to inform him that some local people were very worried because their best sorrel horse had escaped.

A heterogeneous assemblage of objects is to be found not only in the sitting room and the dining room but also in the bathroom.

Antonio's house contains a rich accumulation of objects that he has amassed as a result of his travels, interests, and obsessions, but it is also a sophisticated and thoughtfully arranged stage set "*a la italiana*" in the tradition of those baroque backdrops that accompanied musical

compositions from Monteverdi onward. Running through the center of the extensive estate, which is surrounded by dense pine forest, is a wide access drive with the mural of the angel that prefigures the *leitmotiv* that gives the house its name. Exploiting the unevenness of the ground, Antonio added a conservatory and a greenhouse; these make an interesting walk-through to the swimming pool, which is located in a clearing in the wood; here, on a carpet of pine needles, Antonio decided to install a comfortable and well upholstered couch.

The interior of the house shows off to best advantage his collector's acumen and creative flair. The various rooms run one into the other according to an orthodox classical arrangement; you can almost hear the gentle strains of chamber music that accompany the graceful gestures of waiters going about their business and the tinkle of glasses.

But this initial impression is overlaid by a corrosive, ironic, and nostalgic spirit: there are mirrors that distort perspectives, baroque suns on the ceilings, sculptures that divide space and support false stone arches that might have come from an

imaginary scene by Giulio Romano, polychrome floors, valuable oil paintings that focus the attention, furniture in an endless range of styles that complements this stunning assemblage of items, an environment in which Antonio can relax when he returns from work in his gallery.

Antonio expresses progressive disenchantment with his work, both with regard to the craftsmen who work for him and concerning his clients' tastes. At one time, when there was no competition, carpenters could take their time over their work, and the easy pace of life made for higher standards of workmanship. Added to this, the tastes of his new clients, principally Germans, tend toward a rusticism that is far removed from the subtle and delicate interplay of visual elements that for Antonio is infinitely more valid.

Nevertheless, he is happy to form part of this distinguished company of refined foreigners who inhabit the island, a group of people with very different personalities but who, in his opinion, are not at all provincial. He is also pleased to have had the audacity, with his friend Jörg, to go against the grain of the everlasting

whitewash of the houses, painting them ocher instead. Generally speaking, Antonio endeavors to keep surprises in store for clients and even to surprise himself. His particular sense of irony leads him to mark Sundays and religious festivals by listening to the great masses of Rossini and Verdi. This, he says, brings a smile to the faces of the angels that hover in every corner of the house.

The conservatory provides an ideal transition between the sumptuously decorated rooms of the house and the world outside, where nature is equally exuberant.

Can Torres

When the present owner of Can Torres moved into the property in 1976, there was no electricity; today, by contrast, there is a television in every room. This Milanese extrovert likes to watch any sporting event that is broadcast on satellite television. It was only eight years after moving in that he had a telephone installed – this was obviously well before the invention of the cellular telephone. Up until then, to keep in touch with his friends he would use another method of communication: he would leave messages written on the blue stones that are to be found at the entrance of every house, messages that after a couple of days would produce a reply on his own stone. He had warmed to this pace of life, so far removed from the frenetic pressures of Milan, ever since 1958, when as a hardened yachtsman he had anchored in the capital's little port and, with the wind howling through Sa Peña's deserted streets, had made his way up to El Corsano, the only hostelry for foreigners that there was on the island at that time. The next day, he sailed on a brisk north wind to Formentera. Setting foot on dry land, the only person that he saw was a woman, dressed entirely in black, who was struggling to keep her umbrella upright. Immediately, the sun came out: he had fallen in love with the islands.

He moved into Can Torres and for 22 years owned a fine yacht in which he sailed around the Mediterranean, always returning to his secluded house but alternating those periods of rest and relaxation with unavoidable business trips to Milan. But according to him you cannot sleep in Milan and as the years went by the typical anger of the average Italian toward the politicians who have contributed in fair measure to the degradation of *la bella Italia* has made of him a loner who is only disposed to devote his time to his wife, his friends and a good glass of grappa. And also to Carmen, an

The kitchen, with its old hearth and *trull*, a traditional Ibizan olive press, is replete with an infinite range of home-grown produce and home-made products.

distance and is the regular destination of seaborne expeditions launched by the Italian proprietor, who is also a keen sailor.

The most remarkable feature of the house is what the Ibizans call a "*porxet*," a two-tiered porch which in this particular case has a balcony at the side leading from the bedroom. This creates a remarkable feeling of space that is enhanced by the baldaquin of palm leaves and the enormous flowerpot hanging from the beam of the porch. Everything breathes an air of ease and *joie de vivre*, of a natural lifestyle that is comfortable yet simple, just as the owner wanted, and of which the bougainvillaea, the enormous terra-cotta flowerpots, the great quantity of baskets and other decorative pieces that are dotted about the house form an integral part. Good green vegetables, excellent bread and an Italian pasta that the owner's friends describe as exceptional, are conspicuous in this interior.

Ibizan who, from the time that he first arrived on the island, has been his housekeeper.

Can Torres is one of the oldest houses on Ibiza and its splendid setting, near the Santa Eulalia to Ibiza road, extends southward down to the wide bay and looks out to the horizon. The smooth outline of Formentera can be seen in the

Can Torres, as it is today, is one of the most felicitous examples of an Ibizan house that has been taken over by a foreigner. There is absolute continuity between the original rustic character of the house and the

Above: the typical Ibizan oven built into the porch that leads into the garden. Right: the porch, which traditionally faces south.

lifestyle of its present owner over the last 25 years. The ancient trees of the nearby wood, the palm tree that towers over every Ibizan house meld with the rosebushes and lemon trees that have recently been planted. The asymmetry of the upper porch emphasizes a sophisticated nonchalance; the only contrast is the formality of the bedroom, something that is very Italian. The focal point of the house, however, is the kitchen. On the large dining room table are good cheese and a fine red wine – all that is needed to loosen the tongue of this retired broker, who through tired blue eyes looks out on the world with a mixture of resignation in the face of adversity and a burning desire to live life to the full.

Casa del Elefante

Bruno, a young Frenchman formerly based in Paris, is one of the few owners of the houses that feature in this book to come to Ibiza as recently as the early 1990s. He is fascinated with the motif of the elephant, and this is the theme with which he has decorated a restaurant in San Rafael and with which he is launching a major furniture business, importing some pieces from Indonesia and making others himself.

He has looked to the style of the spectacular murals of the painter Gary Cook, and the result is a decorative scheme that is in a pseudo-vernacular style but that stops short of being excessively rustic and conservative.

Although Bruno is a dynamic businessman, this does not stop him from enjoying good living. His is not a solitary life of contemplation; he prefers to spend his days in Ibiza and his nights out with as many friends as possible. In this sociable spirit he went about finding an old farmhouse where he could put down roots; he found what he was looking for, an isolated property in the pleasant valley that runs between Santa Inés and San Rafael.

The house did not have much land attached but there was enough for what Bruno had in mind: he intended the house to stand in relation to a carefully designed outdoor environment that would consist of terraces, a swimming pool complex, and areas for alfresco meals according to the seasons of the year – in other words, he wanted to create that interchange between the indoor and outdoor aspects of a house that is feasible only in climates such as that of Ibiza. The old house that stood on this site was in total ruin. The original layout of the rooms could be made out only from the rough outline of the walls. The arcades were rebuilt, a feature being made of the capitals on the columns, and wooden beams salvaged from the original structure were used to extend the wings of its pergolas. Spacious new openings were made in the side of the house facing the garden and the swimming pool; this did not alter the outward

The architectural concept of the Ibizan house depends on a close relationship between interior and exterior, between solid forms and space, between windows and interior lighting.

appearance of the building, with its traditional loophole windows, its typically Ibizan roof made of seaweed, ash, and clay, and gargoyles that channel rain water into a cistern. This pleasant outdoor space, above which towers a tall cypress tree, leads on to the walkway toward the

swimming pool. In the manner of a Greek theater, the swimming pool is surrounded by a bowl-like area of land that rises up around it almost like a wall, and is large enough to be laid out in different sections.

After four years, and in keeping with the restlessness of a life divided between Paris and Ibiza, Bruno sold his house. This enabled him to set his sights on finding another property to restore and refurbish, and at the same time made him a handsome profit.

The last addition to be made to the Casa del Elefante was the great Moroccan shop located at one end of the swimming pool; this is the venue for parties, and with the drapes with which it is hung reflected in the water, it is a magical space.

In terms of interior decoration, the Casa del Elefante breaks new ground. This is not a house in which the slow passage of time has left in its wake the trappings of a former lifestyle ingrained with the memories of its earlier inhabitants and filled with treasured possessions brought back from travels or given by friends. It is, by contrast, an interior decorated in a

An easy relationship exists between the traditional and the modern in the bedroom, the kitchen, and the bathroom.

style that has something of the instantaneous snapshot, fixed in a matter of seconds, created by everything from the furniture designed by Bruno to the accompanying paintings and drawings that visitors have left as mementoes on the walls.

We walk away from the house. The road that leads to Santa Inés seems to be colored with the deep enamel-like green of the orange and lemon trees. Bruno's house stands out a little against this green background. It is one of many interesting dwellings that bring this landscape to life. That such a simple entity should be so well suited to its setting is a wonderful thing. One thinks how modern architects of the beginning of the 20th century, full of revolutionary zeal and longing to break with a bourgeois tradition that was stylistically and conceptually bankrupt, latched on to the basic, simple, logical nature of Ibizan architecture, an architecture of the Mediterranean. One also thinks of the architecture of J. A. Coderch, so indebted to all that went before and so fundamental to what was to come afterward. Bruno's house disappears behind lemon trees mottled with yellow, behind the eternal Garden of the Hesperides.

Casa de las Rosas

For all that it is small and architecturally unassuming, the Casa de las Rosas is one of the most sophisticated houses on the island. The owner is an intelligent Italian woman and everything about the house has been thought out in relation to her occupation, something that is not only the apex of professional elitism but also the esthetic and vital lifeblood of her existence. Everything revolves around the cultivation of the rose, the exquisite, poetic flower of Western medieval culture and of the sophisticated Mughal civilization, which once stretched from Persia to Kashmir.

Hundreds of species of rose have taken over the house and garden, and their scent and color invade meadows, wind about trees, and run along pergolas. The interior of the house, decorated in early 20th-century design, is conventional but, unusually, there is a greenhouse attached; made solely of iron and glass, it floods the air with light and continues the horticultural theme. Tucked away in a corner of the bedroom is a workstation; in the elegant disorder mingle the half-dozen books that the owner has written on the subject of roses and which have brought her international fame and renown.

An uncommon modesty, and an understated desire not to make a show, rule in this Ibizan house, which is a world away from others where aspirations to the good life are all too tangibly expressed. The simple, elegant, unassuming nature of the decor, the furniture, and the rooms themselves is evident; only the clearly articulated structure of the greenhouse, the anonymous heir to the tradition of Kew Gardens and Joseph Paxton, has a plainly functional purpose.

The owner of the house once lived comfortably in Milan, where she had connections with the great Italian families, some of whom trace their ancestry back to the popes of the Renaissance and who flaunted their importance and basked in the aura of popular reverence. As the result of unforeseen family problems, she gave up her career in publishing and in 1975 came to Ibiza alone, seeking such a fundamentally different lifestyle that she even considered buying and living on the small uninhabited island of Tagomago, which lies off the northeastern coast

Ibizans who help her and give her advice is very rewarding.

Few people mentioned in this book experience the balanced lifestyle enjoyed by this rose-grower. As the result of her steely determination to establish herself in a new occupation, she has studied rose-cultivation, made trips to England, where rose-cultivation is very highly developed, bought various varieties of rose, and spent long hours preparing and fertilizing the soil, and pruning the roses, all of which has marked her hands and arms with something other than the memory of pretty flowers.

Through the winter, sitting beside the rustic fireplace, she writes her books and in spring enjoys the stimulating, toning, and revitalizing waters of the north coast. She realizes that, with every year that passes, she visits and entertains fewer friends, but at the same time she acknowledges that it is better not to become reclusive. Italian cooking, as her small circle of friends well know, is another great interest of hers, and, as they testify, she pursues it to a very

Roses fill not only the garden (previous page) but also the elegant greenhouse that has been built on to the original house.

of Ibiza. Undaunted by the unique and trying process of buying property, she eventually acquired the farm that included this nameless house, set in the undulating foothills of the Puig d'en Bassettes, on the road to San Miquel.

This is indeed one of the most peaceful parts of the island and one that is blessed with the three attributes that the owner was looking for: tranquility, beauty, and people.

As to tranquility, this Italian woman believes that the island has preserved its identity from earliest times and that the influence of the goddess Tanit transmits this beneficial serenity to her devotees. As to beauty, this is beauty in its widest sense; in things, in counting the passage of time, in the spirit of the place. As to people, she finds that contact with friends, foreign people living on the island, and with native country-dwelling

high standard. Her mother, who comes from an important Italian family, taught her how to make the very best of lightly cooked vegetables and some people compare her gnocchi to the food that the gods in ancient times would have savored in the shade of a Mediterranean vine.

It is now June 1998. It is morning, and as a new day emerges after the fireworks and bonfires of St John's night, the dawn is filled with the scent of the roses that she planted the evening before. The paths all but disappear between the orange, pink, yellow, and white roses that any shah of Shiraz would have grown with the same dedication. The delicate outline of the greenhouse stands out in the dusky dawn. She is at work.

Only a long and thorough exploration would do justice to the variety and beauty of the roses that are to be seen in and around the house.

A Palace in Dalt Vila

Were it not for Dalt Vila, the island of Ibiza would not be what it is, in the same way that Patmos would not be the same without the monastery of St John.

There is positive tension, an active dialectic, in the opposition between the city and the countryside in Ibiza. The Ibizan countryside is not solely a matter of very beautiful landscapes; it is also the repository of authentic Ibizan culture, with its customs, its farmland, its buildings, its music, the entire definition of a place, be that in terms of the whitewashed farmsteads that dot the landscape or acoustically as a territory in which the cry "*uc*" rings out.

The city, La Vila, has from the beginning of time been the center of activity where various cultures have succeeded one another, beginning with its own indigenous rural culture and ending with culture that has arrived from elsewhere. Like every city in the world that has ever existed, La Vila is a place of interchange, of dynamic power, in contrast to the more leisurely pace of

An attractive route leads off the main street in Dalt Vila, to the lobby, and up the steps into the house.

the country. La Vila, in Ibiza, is a remarkable combination of fragments that begins at the marina, taking in Vara del Rey, continues with Sa Peña, and ends at the cathedral-like plateau of Dalt Vila. There, according to the historian Macabich, on its ancient rock, the cults of Bes and Tanit were celebrated. The shrine was superseded in turn by a Roman temple, an early Christian church, an Islamic mosque, and the cathedral that has survived to the present day: the city is an aggregation or palimpsest of cultures.

Just at the place where access from the square leads down to the Calle Mayor, on the spot where the ancient city's highest civic and religious authorities had their headquarters, several small palaces stand side by side between party walls. They were built from the 16th century, at the time when Juan Bautistia Calvi completed the great city walls, the "stone ship," as Antonio Colinas described them.

These houses make up a small block that reaches as far as Sa Portella, the old gatehouse. They stand against the Moorish ramparts and because they are so narrow have the advantage of looking out over two completely contrasting landscapes. The view in one direction is of the narrow stone street that leads up to the cathedral and on up to the castle that towers above the city walls against a patch of blue sky that is constantly strafed by low-flying aircraft as they make their final approach to land near Las Salinas. In the other direction is a breathtakingly beautiful view over the port and the whole island.

Of the three palaces, the one illustrated here has the best-documented connections with nobility. At the time of its most recent restoration, its mysterious well was found to contain old weapons. The well, some 50 feet below the lowest level of the house, is entirely in keeping with the dominant method of construction here, of vertical expansion, with houses that are not particularly large built close together, with a narrow stairway leading up to the flat roof.

It was surely not completely by chance that this fine mansion should have been acquired by an Italian family with connections with the upper echelons of the fashion world. Realizing that the layout of the house was very restricted by the structure of the walls and ceilings, and that the small windows admitted very little light, they decided to rid the interior of incidental furnishings and to create in that unique Dalt Vila house their own Italian interior.

Floors paved with ceramic tiles or with stained wood, and walls smoothed with ivory-colored rendering are the setting for a collection of very high-quality pieces that comprise the interior decor created by this family, from Rome, who discovered Ibiza in the 1960s. Two years of painstaking work have produced an interior in which Roman sculptures and inscribed tombstones, Early Renaissance triptychs and altarpieces, oil paintings, terra-cotta pieces, and carvings, together with fine furniture, complete a highly restrained and elegant whole. Only the wall hangings, bedspreads, and curtains, the specialty of the owners' firm, make a bold splash of color in this interior scheme.

From the restrained dining room, the port of Ibiza can be seen and heard humming with activity, as

Following pages: Furniture in a range of styles, every piece a unique and remarkable example of workmanship, contrasts with the marmoreal whiteness of the statues and stonework.

boats set off for Formentera, each criss-crossing the others' wake while the sun sparkles on the hundreds of white cubes that now pepper the lower levels of the hill behind Talamanca. Through this quiet hum of activity rises the perfume of the oleanders that grow in the little garden beneath the balcony. In December this microcosm will be much calmer and it is then that the owners like to go down to the port and on to Es Vedrà to hear the sound of the sea and the cries of seagulls.

Following pages: the convent of Santo Domingo seen against the backdrop of the city walls, with the port and Talamanca Bay in the background, one of the most beautiful views in Ibiza.

The House of the Indian

It was exactly 100 years ago, at the end of the disastrous war with Cuba (which has always been informally referred to as "the disaster" in Spain), that a doctor of Ibizan extraction felt the call of his native land. Returning to the island, he built himself a house in the colonial style in the open countryside between Ibiza and Santa Eulalia. Following the Caribbean custom, what he built was in fact two houses: a "*casa de labranza*," where the caretaker lived, and a "*casa de recreo*," for himself. While the former was small and modest, the latter was every inch the colonial mansion, built to a symmetrical ground plan, with a grand entrance on the southern side, a palm tree, rush blinds in the windows, and pastel plasterwork, the hallmarks of his Cuban origins.

Exactly 70 years later, the Cuban's granddaughter noticed how various Europeans, people out of the ordinary, were starting to arrive in Ibiza; among those who settled permanently on the island were a couple who had come from rainy Hamburg. The Ibizan-Cuban house, together with the 18 acres that surrounded it, was to be the place that would change their lives. They were delighted that the house should have windows that reached from the floor to the ceiling, just like those in

Hamburg and in complete contrast to the small windows of most Ibizan rural houses.

These two Germans came from backgrounds in the arts and fashion, and although they had pursued different careers their lives had followed parallel paths. He, a lawyer by training, had worked first as a photographer and then later as a journalist whose political commentaries for a certain German television channel are well-known.

On a visit to Spain in 1953, at a time when it was emerging from the postwar years, he had fallen in love with the country, the sun, and the people. When he arrived in Ibiza in 1968 he stayed in El Corsario, the island's only hostelry at that time. He was fascinated by the Phoenician burials that had been discovered in Puig des Molins, in the very heart of the city. Absorbed by the beautiful clay effigies of the goddess Tanit, he had already decided that his future home was to be in Ibiza. He and his partner weighed up and investigated other places where they might find a comfortable life. They love Greece but find the language an insuperable barrier. As their lake in Hamburg froze over, they also considered the

possibility of San Francisco and Bali as their winter quarters. Ultimately, they decided to come and live in the house of the Indian in Ibiza.

The woman, Stefanie Bott, is a cultured and intelligent person who after many years in the fashion business has given free rein to her artistic talents. She has successfully exhibited her work on many different occasions. After a series of very anguished installations, which reflected her harsh perception of reality, she moved in a more surreal direction, taking the familiar image of the mummy, which she made out of bread; it was put on display in a church and eaten by the visitors to the exhibition. Recently she has turned her attention toward photography, focusing mostly on the complex technical processes involved in the superimposition of images.

When they decided to move into their Ibizan house, they knocked down some of the dividing walls. In this Mediterranean setting, the fact that one room leads into the next, the use of dividing doors fitted with glass

The strong, bright Ibizan sunlight is diffused, taking on the palor of the light in northern Europe, homeland of the house's owners.

panels, and the intentionally spartan atmosphere give the house a distinctly Nordic ambience. This is not at all the case outside, where exuberant vegetation and informal bamboo furniture are entirely in keeping with the Mediterranean location of the house.

This Nordic, elegantly Lutheran, almost Bergmanesque quality of the interior is expressed in the rounded outlines of dark wooden furniture, in plain sideboards, in paintings tastefully arranged on classic chimney pieces, in the ubiquitous chandeliers that illuminate the spotless walls and delicate lace curtains. However, even in these immaculate interiors the stamp of the Mediterranean comes as

a welcome contrast: the floors are a brilliantly colorful mosaic typical of late 19th-century Catalan architecture. The mixture of styles that Stefanie and her partner are so fond of is not confined to the interior: parts of the garden further away from the house are laid out in the Oriental manner, with images of Buddha that are visible from many different angles and that remind them of a philosophy of life that they value very highly.

The catamaran that is hidden away behind the house is an outward sign of their love of the sea, of swimming in secluded coves at the quietest times of the year, and of their enjoyment of crossing speedily to

Formentera. The overall impression is that these Ibizans by adoption enjoy enormously the times that they spend in this house, to which they always want to return when their work in Germany allows.

Certain elements of the porch and the garden evoke an Oriental world of serenity and meditation.

Casa de las Tres Lunas

Of the four spits of land that stretch out into the sea on the southern side of the island of Ibiza, pointing toward Formentera, the most accessible and most attractive is Punta Purroig (Red Port), so named for the reddish color of its rocks. This strip of headland has a finger-like point that curves round toward Poniente, forming a sheltered cove that is protected from the blustering winds that batter the east coast at various times of the year. These four spits form a counterpoint to the ravines that cut down to the sea in the inlets and empty the last of the rainfall that collects in the mountainous areas stretching away toward San Josep.

Anyone who has studied, and who can visualize, those places in the western Mediterranean that were colonized by peoples arriving from the East – such as Cretans, Phoenicians, and Greeks – will recognize this piece of land as an ideal location in which to settle. It is south-facing, it commands a clear view out to sea, with beaches for landing, fresh water, and vantage points from which to spot approaching enemies and mount a defense against them. There is indeed a Phoenician settlement on Sa Caleta, a little way east of Purroig. It is open to visitors, and the substantial remains allow a relatively complete picture to be formed of the relationship between these settlers and the landscape. In this imaginative frame of mind, anyone who disembarks at Purroig should not be surprised to find that the cusp of the headland is crowned by one of the most picturesque and atmospheric houses on the island, the House of the Three Moons, built by Rolph Blakstad for a well-known fashion designer. Blakstad is something of an institution in Ibiza and, with Philippe

Rotthier, he has in recent years done much to show Ibizans how the hallmarks of their island identity are descended from a common starting point in antiquity. The two men pursue very different lines of thought. While Rotthier takes a radical and rationalist anthropological approach, Blakstad is a poet and a dreamer, a designer who has such belief in the corpus of theories and legends that built up around the relationship between peoples some 3000 years ago, that he has ended up by creating a syncretic style of architecture that evokes this historic and cultural past.

Turning these ideas into practise, Blakstad has three firm points of departure: an exhaustive knowledge of antiquity gained from those engravings that were the ubiquitous learning aids in all European schools of architecture at the beginning of the 20th century; a clear idea about comfortable living and interior design, derived partly from Arabic traditions; and the backup of specialist craftsmen, who produce the elaborate elements of his designs with all the ease and dexterity of a modern industry. It is these three elements that save his work from falling prey to a decadent kitsch;

moreover, looking beyond any evaluation based on the critique originated by the International Style, his work is undeniably imbued with sensibility and formal brilliance.

Blakstad speaks quietly and deliberately as he shows visitors around the Casa de las Tres Lunas (House of the Three Moons). From what he says he does not seek to arrive at sure and rational conclusions; his statements describe a parabolic trajectory, his narrative a fatalistic accumulation of facts that add up to the evocative and symbolic rather than to the defined and conceptualized. We have barely entered the house and he is speaking with reassuring familiarity of the Solomonic scrolls that adorn the carved stone columns; of the marquetry with symbolic elements relating to the history of the Jews, to Jezebel; of the global inspiration that pervades the whole of Berber art; of the relationship with its ancient Phoenician origins and equally with the goddess Tanit, whose emblem is the three moons.

In barely a murmur that envelops the listener, Blakstad insists on expounding on his theory as if he were a venerable priest reciting

sacred texts. There are only two types of ancestral buildings, he says: houses of the northern countries, built with wooden beams and a sloping roof, and the houses of the arid regions of the south, which have thick walls and are covered with a flat roof to collect rainwater. The synthesis of these two origins gave rise to the Doric temple and the Mesopotamian house.

He runs his hands over the wood – savin wood, the material most extensively used in the House of the Three Moons. He sighs; something that is perhaps not widely known is that savin wood, a type of red cedar, was also the ideal building material in the wadis and fertile areas of Yemen, the region where the Canaanites and the Aramaic civilization formed the original nucleus of Semitic culture, the focal point from which it was to spread out all over the world. Savin wood might have been brought to Ibiza by the Phoenicians.

With an ironic smile Blakstad explains that "Phoenician" in early

Previous page and this page: both the structural and the decorative elements of the house have been designed in a clearly Berber-inspired style.

Roman parlance meant "red people," and later came to be applied to the numerous words with the root "red people" or "red place" that abound in the culture of the arid lands. Purroig is the "red port" where we are now. He continues to speak, ranging over many and different subjects, explaining the difficulty of finding a single material for the walls and floors of the bathrooms, paint-based with epoxy resin, or what is for him the slow technological evolution by which thatched roofs are superseded by tiled roofs.

Blakstad is of Canadian extraction, although his grandparents are able to trace their ancestry back to a noble Viking. When he arrived in Ibiza in 1956 he nursed nebulous ideas about how to build forgotten palaces for other mortals.

The transition between the bedroom and the bathroom evokes the ritual and atmospheric character of Arabic culture.

Vista Hermosa

Of all the houses that feature in this book, it is hard to identify one that stands so firmly at the opposite extreme of what is taken as one of the characteristics of the Ibizan architectural tradition: this is its organic quality, the result of practical considerations and equally of an affinity with nature. Here, in place of naturalness, asymmetry, and economy of movement and materials – everything, that is, that defines Ibizan vernacular architecture – is artifice, symmetry, and a conspicuously liberal use of architectural elements. Yet this house is an example of the taste for the neoclassical style, a preference that is not uncommon among the expatriates that have made Ibiza their home. This universal style, defined by such elements as columns and pediments, has spread throughout the world, so that it may be seen in Miami, on the banks of the Hudson river, in the English counties, or on the outskirts of Paris, and its

building's man façade is a fountain, centered within four grass parterres; sloping lawns define the sides of the house. In complete contrast, the garden, which is better described as a wilderness, is left to its natural state; here are fruit trees that the owner of the house likes to cultivate, and rugged bushes in areas that receive the full summer heat.

Typically of palladian mansions, the interior of the house is laid out as a succession of intercommunicating rooms. The wide passageways are lined with finely proportioned columns and vistas end in imposing marble chimney-pieces over which hang large mirrors that catch the reflection of candelabra, paintings, and gilt chairs.

Palladianism is one architectural style that has spawned an infinite number of variations that are well-suited to their context; in this respect Vista Hermosa stands somewhere between the colonial American and French style. Similarly, the style is also the source of a whole catalog of interior design features, which have

A feeling of control over textures and colors, almost as in a stage or film set, pervades the living rooms and (following page) the bathrooms.

ephemeral presence can also be discerned in that style of avant-garde architecture that goes by the name postmodernism.

Vista Hermosa is a house that is perfectly suited to the purpose for which it was built – the home of a famous German actress who uses it all year round, especially in winter,

when in the rest of Europe temperatures sink to their annual low. Revealingly, being newly-built in an ostensibly alien style, this house needs a suitable backdrop of rough ground in order make it blend into the Ibizan hills that border the road running from La Vila to Santa Eulalia. At the foot of the stairway on the

become totally internationalized and which in the case of this house are used with exquisite good taste.

The owners of Vista Hermosa divide their time between leisurely strolls in the countryside and entertaining guests, hosting dinners for several dozen people at a time. On those occasions, the elegantly furnished interiors of the house come to life, taking on the spirit of the period movies in which the owner has appeared in the course of her professional career.

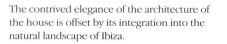

The contrived elegance of the architecture of the house is offset by its integration into the natural landscape of Ibiza.

The Golden Section

In 1984 a German advertising copywriter came to Ibiza and Formentera, places that immediately went to the top of the list of dream locations where he might come and live to get away from the stress and strain of his working life. Alongside more exotic possibilities, Ibiza emerged the clear favorite both because it is easier to reach from Germany and on account of its wonderful climate.

Methodically, the German went about searching for possible locations for a new house that an architect friend of his would design for him. The choice was governed largely by the desire for a view directly onto the sea, and was further narrowed down by the need for the house to command a view that was sufficiently inspiring to satisfy his demanding creative talent. After a typically exhaustive search, he obviously found not only what he was looking for but, as he says, better than he could have dreamed: Cala Carbó is one of those small secluded coastal villages that lie on Ibiza's western side, along the wide strip of coastline that runs from San Antonio Bay to Cabo Llentrisca. These two pieces of headland tail off into clusters of small

islands, those at San Antonio being known as La Cunillera and those just off the small reef as Es Vedranell, which includes an impressive outcrop of rock named Es Vedrà.

As far as its size and shape are concerned, Es Vedrà has everything that the most demanding late 18th-century Romantic landscape painter could want. It rises steeply from the sea, with two spits of rock receiving the full force of the wind and waves; looking at it, it is easy to lose a sense of time and scale, so that it appears supernatural and hauntingly beautiful. According to tradition, this mysterious island was inhabited by a well-known hermit; today it is populated by wild goats, and has been singled out by the German copywriter as the setting for his new home.

His architect understood his needs perfectly, and within two years the house had been completed. It was built of metal and glass, simple materials, yet radically different from the traditional Ibizan stone and lime. The style of the house is in the German rationalist tradition, with the

The magical transition between the entrance hall, the sitting room, the swimming pool, and Es Vedrà, the rock.

Fatamorgana

The typical Ibizan rural house is a whitewashed building that stands in isolation in the landscape. But there are three homesteads on the island, located in the foothills of mountains in the San Lorenzo area, that are exceptional in that they form a cluster of buildings. Of the three – Balafi, Atzaro, and Morna – the best known is Balafi, or Balafia. With its cylindrical defensive towers marked with curious signs, it is one of the most unique buildings on Ibiza.

Like the other homesteads, Balafi consists of a nucleus of five houses that were jointly fortified against attack. To a greater or lesser degree, each house displays the typically Ibizan tendency to grow outward; what is unusual, however, is the resulting complexity of this homestead, with some buildings almost melding into one another and others virtually touching across a space or narrow alleyway. The resulting cluster of shapes makes for a very picturesque whole, unified by the whitewash that covers most of the walls; with the three cylindrical towers that rise up like spurs, it also has a very distinctive appearance. A host of other buildings, such as corrals, bakehouses, and toolsheds,

are piled around the main buildings and create that homogeneity typical of vernacular architecture, broken only by the rich brown of the natural stone of the towers.

It is only to be expected that such an expert as Rolph Blackstad, who over the course of 30 years has acquired an intimate knowledge of every corner of Ibiza, should have a special fondness for such a remarkable example of vernacular architecture. When in 1990, after a long search, a Dutch couple who had settled in Ibiza in 1973 asked him to build them a house in the shadow of Balafia, he probably had mixed feelings. On the one hand, the sheer

size of the projected house would rival that of the cluster of buildings comprising Balafia, each spoiling the other's commanding position in the landscape. On the other hand, Blakstad's particular attitude sees the Ibizan architectural tradition as a stylistic continuum, a synthesis between Greek and Arabic styles, the two most prominent architectural styles to pervade the Mediterranean. Taking into account how meticulously Blakstad has analyzed Ibizan architecture, this attitude differs from the more objective approach that, making less reference to history, focuses more directly on the methods by which Ibizan houses are built.

It is difficult to be sure whether this was precisely the architect's thinking when his client asked him to design a large house with a courtyard as its focal point; this feature was intended to make the most of the high ground that commanded prime views over Levante, Garbi, and Tramontana. The courtyard and the rooms leading off it were to take the shape of a large cross lying on the flattened summit of the hill.

To avoid exposing the house to the risk of fire, part of the wood was

cleared. The resulting space was turned into an elaborate Moorish garden that counterbalanced the swimming pool and that consisted of a bank of aromatic plants in front of the house, the south-facing aspect where the main rooms are located.

To first-time visitors, the house appears strikingly impressive, as the friendly owner welcomes them in the courtyard that functions both as the main entrance and the fulcrum that gives access to all parts of the building. The courtyard is a reproduction, possibly an exact one, of the courtyard of the mosque of Zebid, that small village in Yemen that is reputedly the birthplace of algebra and the location that Pasolini chose to shoot *The Thousand and One Nights*. The courtyard contains a fountain of Mughal inspiration and a series of white marble waterspouts that might have come from Granada's monumental Alhambra.

This was the dream house where the owner planned to live all year round. The architect fulfilled the brief with great creative flair and technical skill. Not unexpectedly, the dream

The warm night air fills the calm expanse of the spacious Arab-inspired patio.

The layout of its component parts and the manipulation of light give this great mansion its eastern character.

was difficult to maintain in certain areas of the house; thus the rigidity of the ground plan affects the layout of the living room and comfort is sometimes sacrificed to a structure that is somewhat inflexible.

Blakstad's creative genius also comes to the fore in the design of the garden. Exploiting the lie of the land as much as the shape and size of the various elements, he has created an evocatively Moorish garden, where water plays a major part in the architectural scheme.

In El Puig de Sa Bassa

The sun beats down upon the pine trees, cicadas thrum, and an acrid smell of flowering shrubs pervades the air. Anyone who climbs the foothills of Sa Talaia de San Carles will experience the heady force of this environment. A few steps more and an enchanted place comes into view: a great expanse of concrete, defined by two bare walls, and beyond a collection of concrete sculptures, ascetic and abstract, angular yet soft in outline; though enclosed within this artificial environment, they sit perfectly against their background – woodland and a blue horizon that stretches to infinity. Here is the studio of another of those unusual people who have made Ibiza their home.

From the top of the hill, the location of this sculptor's remarkable studio, an old house can be seen nestling in the folds of the hill further down to the south. This is El Puig de Sa Bassa, where the sculptor lives with his wife and daughter. The house is surrounded by orchards, while untrammeled nature runs riot in the rest of the garden.

The sculptor comes from a Milanese family who trace their origins back to the 16th century. As a

young man he had wide interests, including sport, literature, and ultimately sculpture. He studied ethnology in the heyday of the French Levi-Straussian school and from the 1950s his knowledge of African art (of Mali, Upper Volta, Cameroon, Nigeria, and so on) wrought a permanent link between anthropology and sculpture, the two subjects that he found most absorbing. While sailing around the Mediterranean he had once put into port at Ibiza, but it was not until 1974 that he settled permanently on the island. He and his wife were enchanted by the sense of history that pervades the Ibizan landscape. Over several visits to the island they went about searching for the rural house that they longed for. They purchased El Puig from a German and moved into the house in 1979, even though it was virtually unfurnished. Since 1982 the sculptor's house has become a comfortable place to live in, and in it are now displayed his important collection of African artifacts, alongside his own work, an unusual combination of objects that pervade the whole house.

The sculptor and his family have not severed links with their previous

life, however; he continues to exhibit his work, to write articles for *La Corriere de la Sera*, and to support ethnological museums in Italy; his daughter, based in this house in Ibiza, works as a graphic designer, sending her work to her international clients by electronic means. In Ibiza the sculptor has found a tangible yet indefinable mix of elements: light, silence, the existence of manual labor, a taste for natural things, the rhythm of life, the absence of consumerism, beauty that lies in the smallest and simplest things.

He and his wife have not altered the old house at all, preserving intact the dining room with its great wall clock, the bakehouse, the arcades and compounds. But they built a new addition, constructed of stone from the quarries of San Carles, which seamlessly abuts the house beneath an exuberant growth of bougain-villaea and wisteria.

They value all that the island holds for them and lament developments that have scarred tourist areas, places beyond their

The interior decoration of the house revolves around the alternation between African sculpture and pieces created by the owner himself.

enchanted hinterland. They dream, a special dream among Ibizan dreams, of a simple, well-ordered world in which work and life are one, the world known to Dolo Bara, the Dogon chief, in his village in Bandiagara gorge, when they lived in Mali. Perhaps because of this, the house is not arranged, furnished, or decorated in any distinctive or ostentatious way. Its ordinariness derives from the lifestyle of its inhabitants. In this normal, even perhaps neutral, environment, the African sculptures, together with his own, stand out in singular contrast; it is as if the inhabitants of the house wish to see them as the talisman that

As in all Ibizan houses, staggered successions of outbuildings is attached to the main house. Here, they culminate in the open-air workshop of the sculptor who owns the house.

has allowed them to understand life and creativity. These sculptures are treated as part of the furniture, as if to show that their importance springs from the fact that they are integral to their creator's philosophy of life. Asked which artists have influenced him, he names Brancusi without hesitation but also invokes the anonymous carvers of Cycladic figures, the many and nameless Romanesque painters, and Paolo di Domo, that self-effacing artist known as Paolo Ucello.

El Mosquetero

From three points of the compass, the city of Ibiza has its familiar appearance, a neat and picturesque entity nestling in the landscape. On the side that straggles outward toward Poniente, however, it becomes an unsightly suburb, where well-proportioned, harmonious, and sundrenched buildings give way to an agglomeration of ugly shapes. No one would imagine that an artist would live in such an environment, and that by drawing inspiration from the very soullessness of the district he should have created such a highly imaginative living space. To counter the limitations of so restricted a space, this artist has created optical illusions, and by breaking all the rules of style and good taste he has proclaimed his independent and cosmopolitan spirit.

Olivier Mourao is a Brazilian painter who, soon feeling restricted in his own country, set off on his travels to broaden his artistic perspective. He considers that young painters of the late 19th-century were fortunate in being able to go on a Grand Tour, an instructive journey that opened out their artistic vision. In his view, those who benefited most from the experience were the English, who had the knack of observing and assimilating a variety of styles, cultures, and ways of life. Olivier, who defends to the hilt the mannerisms of his style, repudiates the dictum "less is more" that pervades almost all 20th-century art. For him London is the ideal place to be, somewhere that offers quality in quantity and the most sophisticated

lifestyles. But Ibiza is ultimate freedom, the necessary antidote to English formality and formalism.

The painter decided to live in Ibiza for the warmest months of the year. The rest of the time he works in England. In this way his creativity alternates between periods of time devoted to making preparatory drawings and producing paintings on canvas. Unlike other people who own houses in Ibiza, Olivier has no desire to live a quiet, secluded life; he wants constant contact with people, with his friends, mostly on the beach or in the discotheque. He sees his house as an extension of this sociable life, peopled by forms that run the gamut from realistic to surreal, an unrelated assortment of objects that add up to a visual cacophony. For Olivier, this superabundance, overdesign, and accumulation of objects embodies the heterogeneity that he sees as tremendously positive and as forming the basis of creativity in the present day. In his opinion, Ibiza has this mixture of people, languages, customs, and so on; it springs from the very strong spirit of place and of metaphysical nature that the island exudes and that has valuable therapeutic properties.

For these vital reasons, Olivier expressly wished to flout the conventions of the ideal living space – something that is sought by most foreign people in Ibiza. He picked the least inspiring district of the city and within six years had methodically decorated his house, fashioning an enclosed world whose only limits are his fertile imagination. The property's

conventional walls were torn down and the terrace was altered; out of this emerged a new environment defined by a complex and ground-breaking *trompe l'oeil*.

For Olivier, there is a perfect formal continuity between his house and the interior of Pacha, the discotheque whose hybrid house music fills an unreal space with glittering darkness.

The manipulation of space, the use of *trompe-l'oeil*, the superimposition of pictorial effects in the interior decoration, unexpected juxtapositions and the evocative power of colors and shapes have resulted in the creation of an unusual world in a conventional apartment.

Memphis House

José is one of the most typical people from the world of fashion in Ibiza. His shop, The End, located off the marina in the city of Ibiza, has been a landmark since the 1960s; more than a purely commercial enterprise, it attained the status of fashion icon.

In 1982 José built himself a house in Can Martinet, where an older building already stood. His aim was to build simple and functional living quarters around a central space in which the swimming pool was to be located. A series of shallow openings and overhead lighting wells provided the play of light and shade that is so typical of contemporary architecture.

In the 1970s the house, which stands in a large agricultural estate,

was the venue of a great may all-night parties; the flames of many torches would illuminate suntanned flesh, some of it clothed only in undulating and multicolored body paint. In latter years, José explains, these parties have tailed off because of the excessive increase in the number of visitors.

For the sake of coherence, considering the materials with which the original house was built, the existing ground plan was not changed. Moreover, the chimneys, mantelpieces, and windows of the main rooms were left intact so as to preserve the original appearance of the interior.

José decided that the decoration of the house should be object-based, featuring works by his artist friends, such as Gustavo Elorriaga. This was in the days when the artist Ettore Sottsass and his Memphis Group were at the height of their powers, when the radical antimodernist style was catching on, and when Alssandro Mendini launched the magazine *Domus*. It was also the time when Mariscal and the designs of Eduardo Samso were becoming familiar to the general public and had begun to exert a strong influence on

Barcelona as it was before the city hosted the 1992 Olympic Games.

In this house, whose doors are permanently open to visitors, José has worked for the great international fashion retailers, putting together collections and packing off consignments of clothes. As a result of all this, Memphis House is anything but quiet and homely; nor is it bathed in the folklorism with which most Ibizan houses are imbued. The whole atmosphere of this house, which has a very public feel, is something midway between an art gallery and an upmarket fashion store, and there the owner finds a perfect balance between his lifestyle and his creative profession.

Modern European building techniques combined with traditional Ibizan materials create a minimalist interior in which sculptural objects obey a strictly ordered counterpoint.

The porches of the house become windows
that admit light and frame the expanse of water
of the swimming pool.

Can Micali

The northwestern side of Ibiza has a distinctive character. The area is bounded by the San Antonio and San Miquel roads; and perhaps because of the lie of the land, of the rugged outline of the Aubarca coast, as well as the great size of the houses and the absence of urban agglomerations, it has something grandiose about it. Not that this landscape is unappealing, especially in the low-lying areas that are irrigated by watercourses and laid out to extensive orange, lemon, lime, and pomegranate plantations, and vineyards. This is the most unspoilt area of the island, and here there are unmodernized rural houses, many of them still inhabited by Ibizan peasants, others standing empty and in ruins. In one of those valleys, scarred by the markings of an old quarry, stands the house of a well-known German sculptor whose work is displayed in many museums and galleries of contemporary art; it also graces the grounds of his Ibizan farmstead, creating a striking outdoor environment.

This artist came to Ibiza as a student in 1953, and fell profoundly in love with the island, so that after touring the rest of the Mediterranean

he decided to return here. The experience of staying in various rural houses fired his enthusiasm to settle permanently in Ibiza; it also affected his work, which became touched by the mythical atmosphere of Ibiza and the inescapable relationship with the sun. Life in Ibiza was beginning to have a profound impact on him, and over the years he amassed first-hand information about life in the countryside and took hundreds of photographs that went to make up the subject of an important book that was recently published. Given his attachment to the island, he was very

particular about his choice of a permanent residence. After having viewed close to 40 old houses, he finally found what he was looking for in the most unspoilt area of the island, between Santa Inés and Santa Gertrudis; this was a pine forest in which, on the edge of the abandoned mine, stood an unusual peasant dwelling that commanded a magnificently extensive view. Unusually, the layout of the house consisted of one large room, with a porch, two rooms at the rear, and various other rooms on both sides. It was south-facing, and set up against the rise of the hill for shelter from the north wind.

After certain modifications and enlargements, the sculptor made his studio in the western part of the house, which overlooks the sheer drop of the quarry and faces a level area of land where his sculptures are set out. The eastern part of the house consists of a comfortable suite of rooms, made pleasant to live in both through the chill of winter and in the heat of summer, and ends with a

The restrained outline of the house contrasts with the lushness of the landscape.

floods into every room. The dream of this particular Ibizan householder is the same as the dream that evolved in the minds of architects and other artists at the beginning of the 20th century – namely the realization that vernacular architecture, particularly in Ibiza, with its organic capabilities and economy of design, could be adapted to the practical and esthetic needs of modern houses.

This mode of living has allowed many adoptive Ibizans to achieve their ideal: to find fulfillment, to work and live in a privileged location, and to find contentment.

flight of steps leading to the large swimming pool which stands sharply defined in the noonday sunlight. To the north of the swimming pool is a pavilion that also acts as a dividing wall, continuing westward and preventing earth from piling up against the house, as it had done in the past. For the sculptor, who lives in the house with his wife and daughter, restoring the building was an architectural labor of love. He used reclaimed beams, doors, and flooring, authentic furniture and household equipment, and old agricultural tools; some of these he has turned into inspired pieces of sculpture, which decorate the attractively designed interior that is bathed by the filtered white light that

Various pieces of sculpture fashioned from traditional everyday objects made by Ibizan craftsmen.

The rectangular form of the swimming pool,
and the palm trees are characteristic of the
Mediterranean Arabic tradition.

La Colmena

North of the city of Ibiza, beyond the Llano de Jesús, the road leads up to Roca Llisa golf course, whose green for most of the year is anything but verdant – this type of vegetation, at the mercy of the dry Mediterranean climate, is not best suited to such a typically British sport.

Like any smart golf course, Roca Llisa has an agglomeration of buildings; the finest of these is a cluster of staggered apartments, a type of development that surely has less impact on the environment than the identical individual houses that swarm over every cove on Ibiza's eastern coast. In this cluster of small apartments, with neat balconies oriented toward Formentera, lives a man who loves antiques and works in the antiques business.

Like many foreign people who live in Ibiza, he first came to the island as a young man. Then, the only places to stay were in the as yet unspoilt San Antonio Bay, and rooms in the Bahia Hotel cost less than 100 pesetas a night. He stayed there for three months, and then decided to return and settle there permanently if he could find suitable work.

His interest in antiques led him into a job. When he first realized that a pair of carved wooden cherubs that he had picked up at auction could be resold at a profit in Switzerland, he decided to establish himself as an antiques dealer. In London, the center of the European antiques business, he gained the kind of experience that made him one of the most knowledgeable operators in the antiques field.

He devoted much thought to the best location for his future house. He bought a plot of land in San Miquel, considered a fine country house in Dalt Vila, and finally turned down the opportunity of acquiring a mansion in one of the best developments near Cala Molí. His pragmatism steered him toward one of the small apartments in the agglomeration at Roca Llisa, which had the virtue of anonymity and luxury. The small enclosed environment – a suite of

exquisitely decorated rooms – that he has created is unknown to all but a few of his neighbors. To create what he had in mind, he converted the apartment into virtually a single room that, cleverly leading straight onto the balcony, makes for the greatest feeling

of space. This impression of space, which, surprisingly, is emphasized by the surviving columns and load-bearing walls, points towards the strong yet subtle relationship between compartmentalized interiors and the great outdoors.

His second major decision was to paint the whole apartment in a single color, a sophisticated reddish purple, which gives it the appearance of an art gallery. Here are displayed Roman busts, whose pale yet resplendent tone harmonizes with the warmth and nobility of the Georgian furniture. A small brazier made of shells introduces an exotic touch and melds with pieces in the Art Deco style; and in the center of the room stand large Indonesian wooden chests and cherry-red vases that echo the color of the walls.

The owner's individual sense of space and form is what makes this scheme work. The finishing touch is the way in which the balcony is integrated into the living space; the boundary between indoor and

By removing partition walls, the owner has created a single unified space, making of his apartment an ideal environment in which to display the artistic treasures that he has accumulated.

outdoor is blurred with the disposition of plants inside and fine carpets outside. Spreading out in the open air, the elements are separated only by a door that inexorably reflects the azure of sea and sky.

Filled with indoor furniture and decorated with the same materials as the living room, the terrace forms a direct link between the interior of the house and the landscape round about, and a vista that reaches right out to the hazy outline of Formentera.

Can Colomer

The dialectical relationship between town and country is very apparent in certain areas of Ibiza; these are basically agrarian districts, however, over time, and thanks to a certain type of incoming resident, they have taken on a markedly modern urban appearance.

This unique relationship between indigenous inhabitants and foreign incomers (among whom must even be counted Catalans) is now well established, and the resulting mix has contributed to the formation of an environment that, in social terms, is markedly different from the original, preexisting rural culture. The village of San Carlos is one those places in which a very vigorous rural sector coexists side by side with a lifestyle that is fundamentally different. The area around San Carlos is an unusually attractive plain dotted with small hillocks, sheltered from the north wind by the Sierra de San Vicente and El Puig de Sa Sabina. At the junction between the Santa Eulalia to San Vicente road and the highway that links the center of the island with its eastern coast, stand a number of hamlets and the village of San Carlos itself; in this agglomeration there has existed for

some years a unique urban culture, the hallmarks of which are the Dalias street market, the bars of San Carlos, the school for foreign children, shops, and so on.

In this setting, dominated by the measured rhythm of agricultural labor, in the heart of a countryside punctuated with pine-covered hills, stands Can Colomer, the old farmhouse where Carlos Martorell lives for several months over the summer. Carlos Martorell is a Barcelona man through and through, and he breathes the culture of his native city, exuding a cosmopolitan nature and that image of the modern metropolis that the world at large has of Spain's second city since it hosted the Olympic Games. Even before that, in the legendary 1960s, Carlos belonged to a group of culturally adventurous people who in the popular imagination were identified with Bocaccio, the nightclub run by Oriol Regás. Since those days Carlos has worked variously as an advertising agent and organizer of major social events, and is also the author of art books and videos.

Carlos Martorell first became acquainted with Ibiza at an early age, even before a wave of hippy culture descended on the island, and he had once lived in a little house in the village of San Jordi, near to the airport, in the shadow of the singularly attractive fortified church. A few years later he bought a fisherman's cottage from a gypsy woman; it faced onto Sa Carrosa, the fine promenade that leads up from the harbor and along to Dalt Vila, in the island's capital, and from this pied-à-terre he set about fixing up Can Colomer.

What he liked about this house was its unusual setting, on a hill encircled in the manner of a crater by carob trees, almond trees, and pines. In this completely rural setting the simple white outline of the building follows the organic layout of old Ibizan houses, stretching away until it melts into the almond trees and fig trees, heavy with fruit. The house has kept all its original features, from the thatched roof, made up of an insulating mixture of reeds, seaweed, and mud, to the savin beams, and the weather-beaten eaves at the entrance.

Inside the house Carlos Martorell has left intact the great chimney-piece; the hearth is surrounded by whitewashed stone seats and has stone flooring worn smooth by centuries of

Previous page and this page: a sophisticated
and relaxed treatment of the outbuildings.

use. In another room a carved wooden bench covered in cushions creates a simple yet luxurious atmosphere of comfort, which is enhanced by the golden glow of candles, the only source of light in this room. Beyond, a mirror reflects back an image of a white-painted bedroom hung with plain curtains.

Not surprisingly, the owner lives in this setting in a voluntarily primitive state, which he paradoxically values as a luxury on a par with that of the most sophisticated hotel. A series of purifying rites – drawing water from the well, shaving in the shade of the carob tree, pulling on a white Moroccan robe, feeding the geese, or gathering the first of the early figs in June – has become for him a fundamental part of the process of mental relaxation that he seeks.

From this peaceful and well-aspected position, Carlos Martorell declares himself open to ways of living that bring continuous change and unlimited possibility, the two things that most interest him.

The interior of the old house has been left practically untouched. The pebble flooring is especially interesting.

Every detail of the interior scheme displays a profound elegance, which is rooted both in Ibizan tradition and in the style of the late 1970s disseminated by the Catalan architectural avant-garde, from José Luís Sert to J. A. Coderch.

The House that Springs from the Earth

In one of the little blind valleys that run up into the foothills between the San José road and the coves of the southern coast stands a newly-built house. Deeply set into the hillside, with dry-stone walls built in local stone, it is all but invisible to anyone passing by on the road.

It all began almost 30 years ago, when a German architect, overwhelmed by the pressures of his working life, began to question his lifestyle (he worked near Frankfurt) and spent four years in Ibiza, during which time he enjoyed a completely different lifestyle, living in an old farmhouse in San Agustín. He spent some time deciding whether his permanent residence was to be a converted Ibizan homestead or a completely new house; he finally opted for the latter, adding to the plans a small study for his work. His decision to relocate coincided with the advent of fax machines and electronic mail.

On this basis he began looking at Ibizan construction methods and the need, in the highly self-critical context of his former working environment, for sustainable housing that was suited to its environment. The ever-increasing legal restrictions

and technological demands in Germany seemed to him like a one-way street; by contrast, the opportunity to experiment in Ibiza with a style of architecture that is economical in the widest sense of the word opened up a whole new window on his profession. In his studio in Ibiza the plans that he has drafted in minute detail are for new types of houses that will be built in Croatia and the United States; their curved stone walls, like those of his house in Ibiza, both define the living space and graduate the entry of light.

The restricted space in the valley where his house is built limits the dimensions of the building. The curved outer wall has produced a circular dwelling that is centered on the nucleus of the kitchen and bathroom, but that is open on the two sides where the living room and the dining room are located.

Fluid space, light that enhances textures and interiors, the attractive contrast between exposed stonework and wooden beams, characterize this part of the house. A second building,

The unified nature of the living space and the voluptuousness of its furnishings harmonize with the organic nature of traditional Ibizan interiors.

countryside. Breathing in deeply, the owner, another of those people who have fallen in love with the island, affirms that Ibiza possesses an indefinable magic that has a beneficial effect on anyone who lives there. This is why his house stands deeply rooted in the land, and why for him it is a haven that provides shelter from heat and cold, and also perhaps a place where he can tune in to the island's spirit.

set in front and at a slightly lower level, contains guest rooms and the swimming pool, which is also circular and which acts as an extension to the main part of the house. The third tier takes the form of a garden, which the owner would like to integrate more closely with the wooded area that surrounds the house. The valley, a natural continuation, disappears down to the sea. The owner plans to moor the boat that he is about to acquire next to the local fishing boats, in the stone and wooden harbors that fan out spontaneously in the little neighboring coves.

The late summer light bathes the stone with a warm earth color. Only the blue water of the swimming pool stands out against the tranquil

The double spiral staircase leads up to a mezzanine where the bedroom is located. The bathroom is enclosed within the circular stone tower.

Can Kali

First impressions are of penetrating blue-gray eyes, a forehead with the Hindu red mark, and a persuasive tone of voice that insists on complete anonymity: this is the owner of Can Kali, an imaginative and radical conversion of a late 18th-century rural Ibizan house. It stands halfway up the side of a deep valley, midway between the skyline and the dark dampness of the gorge that scores the valley, and comes into view at the end of a lengthy ride along a winding road that hugs the pine-covered hillside. This man, softly spoken and out of the ordinary, starts to open up as he speaks of his arrival in Ibiza 1972, almost by accident, as the result of a difficult personal decision after having come through hard times.

The break with a previous life, including the comforts and conveniences of Western civilization, the abandonment of his career as an architect, the quest for a new identity and for spiritual and physical renewal, occupied him in the early stages of his Ibizan odyssey. This fundamental life change was the path chosen by a thoughtful and cultivated personality, equally receptive to the premises of Western thought, which spring from the Platonic ideal, and to the powerful spirituality of Hinduism, with its deeply ingrained sincerity

Can Miquel
de Sa Font de Morna

The cluster of houses at Morna nestles in a fertile, sun-drenched valley above which rises the outline of Puig des Fornàs. Past Can Lluquí, the road that runs along the valley starts to climb up toward a much steeper area where Can Miquel de Sa Font stands. The house dates from 1822, and during the course of the

rebuilding work that Rolph Blakstad carried out in 1969, a quantity of Roman coins were discovered buried beneath the living area, proof positive that this exact site has been inhabited off and on since antiquity.

The house is laid out along typical Ibizan lines, and descends in stages southward. Blakstad added the large complex formed by the swimming pool and fountain, and converted the interior so as to create a larger living room. In this house Blakstad was able to concentrate on those aspects that most challenge and interest him personally: a comfortable interior, the relationship between the interior and the exterior of the house, and the manipulation of light. In this house the architect felt under no obligation to pull off the architectural and

stylistic tours de force that his clients have demanded of him over the last few years, and which can sometimes result in the creation of excessively picturesque confections.

With Can Miquel, there was no need for Blakstad to comply with an overambitious project. To his great satisfaction, what came to the fore here was all that he has absorbed over the years about two basic aspects of architecture – Ibizan building techniques and the historical tradition of villages of the arid zones, basically that of Arabic culture.

For Blakstad, the adaptation of a particular architectural style to a particular geographical context, in this case Ibiza, is something that is dictated not so much by climate as by culture; in this respect, when he builds in Ibiza, he designs along the lines of what could be described as an architecture of the south, an historical-cultural entity whose extent and fabric have been validated by thousands of years of history. Blakstad insists that authentic Ibizan

The rounded forms of Ibizan vernacular architecture are effectively combined (following page) with the refinement of Arabic elements.

culture is a rural culture, and that Ibizan architecture has not changed since remote times; he believes that these great timespans, or historical interstices, are marked by cultural exchange, major migratory movements, or nomadic and trading routes, that forge links between such distant places as North Africa and the easternmost reaches of the Silk Route. Blakstad is drawn ever deeper into exploring the ancient origins of architecture. He has established a foundation in Vancouver whose purpose is to trace the common roots of domestic architecture.

Sitting chatting in the living room of Can Miquel, he laments the fact that the International Style of architecture, albeit for perfectly acceptable ideological reasons, has severed all links with the past. Meanwhile dusk is falling and golden light penetrates the corners of the room; it is subdivided into smaller spaces, an arrangement that can be seen in the living quarters of the Alhambra, where spaces are defined by very slight unevennesses in the floor that are analogous to the edges of thick carpets.

As doves flutter into the farmstead, light from the windows projects their outline in fantastic silhouette. A small Moorish lantern glowing at ground level in a corner of the room sends fine rays of light onto the inlaid ceiling.

Outside, horseshoe arches define the elongated fountain into which water tumbles from two spouts in a typically Moorish floral formation. Beyond, the pavilion beneath palm trees, is laid out ready for dinner. Marjorcan glass goblets catch the last of the sunlight and the dates and mandarins glow in the semidarkness that engulfs the Morna valley.

The final question, prompted by the overhead light, leads Blakstad on to another historical fact: how in warmer parts of the world light filters

The mild Ibizan climate allows the creation of exterior living spaces in the magnificent tradition of the Alhambra in Granada.

through wells and courtyards and how, in certain Aryan cultures, the beam of natural light falls onto the hearth, so that the place where there is fire and light is symbolically one and the same.

The architect's voice takes on that drowsy tone that is habitual with him when he speaks at length: "In Mycenaean palaces the hearth was typically located in the center of the building, and this is just what happens in the farmhouses and palaces of Nurestan or Bactria. Alejandro Magno has traced common denominators between all these cultures and identified a common place of origin for the whole of Aryan culture: this is Balkh, the capital of an empire that is completely unknown today, the birthplace of Zoroaster, the god who lit up the earth with fire."

The swimming pool takes the form of a rectangular Moorish-style pool, with superb views in two directions.

Can Embarcador

Haussmann, and Le Corbusier with a long line of Catalan architects that begins with José Luís Sert and Rodriguez Arias, continues with J. A. Cordech, and culminates with the contemporary Ibizan architect Elias Torres. While the style that is derived from the initial Rationalist movement is clearly perceptible in the development of Catalan architecture, this is not true of the modern movement in Madrid; although the latter was also influenced by the strict geometric proportions of peasant houses, be they Ibizan or Andalucian, it sought elsewhere the stylistic elements that distinguish it from the tradition that is identified as Catalan. Miguel Fisac, one of the most important architects of the Madrid school in the years after the Spanish Civil War, introduced into his interesting works elements of a language whose origins lay as much in Scandinavian Neo-classicism as in the ambiguous canons of Italian fascism, particularly in the repetition and deformation of arches.

In the 1930s in Ibiza there developed a cultural symbiosis between the centuries-old rural building style of the island and a new architectural style that, originating in Germany, was soon to be universally known as Functionalism, and which led in turn to the International Style. This trend linked such major European architects as Brönner, One of the first modern houses (as opposed to apartment blocks) that were built in Ibiza soon after the Spanish Civil War was that which the decorator, architect, and aristocrat

Javier de Olaso built for himself. In this house the recurring theme is the square arch, defined by a plain molding, very similar to those used by Miguel Fisac. A series of such arches surrounds the house, marking the boundary with sky and sea, pierced by the little islands of Es Bosc and S'Espart, opposite Cala Conta.

The significance of Olaso's building lies in the fact that he took into account the unevenness of the rocky outcrop on which it was to stand, laying out a sequence of stepped platforms that accentuated its artifice and geometry. On this original base he placed the columns, which subtly create a boundary between the outside terraces and the split levels within. The house is so narrow and wide that it could be seen as a single very thick wall. This feature makes possible one of the most elegant aspects of its design – a direct visual link between the back of house, where a doorway opens out onto Cala Conta, and the front, with the main entrance.

Can Embarcador is one of the Ibizan houses which has the most favorable setting in relation to the sea. Its terraces enclose living areas, the swimming pool, and a series of walkways that descend toward the old fishermen's jetty (*embarcador*) for which the house is named. Olaso decked out the interior with a carefully chosen selection of assorted objects, pieces of furniture that are also sculptures; these are displayed in an immaculate white space, enhanced by a series of light wells that run parallel to the blind wall on one side of the house.

A few years ago this estate was acquired by another of the people who belong to the group of sophisticated foreigners that live on the island. He is the archetypal Italian, someone that one can picture in Milan or Turin, the chairman of a major industrial concern, who is equally at home on the deck of a yacht, big-game hunting in Uganda or Mozambique, or on a sophisticated beach on Bali. Congenially, and poking fun at himself, he relates his erratic pilgrimage to New York, the seven years that he spent as a sculptor in Bali, and the African big-game hunting episodes in the days before the invasion of the package-tour wildlife safari.

He has achieved his personal ambition of traveling the world and possibly he has still not found what

The splendid location on a cliff overlooking the sea at Poniente provided the starting point in the conception of this modern house.

he has been looking for. Born in the narrow strip of territory between Italy and Croatia, he feels himself a man of the frontier who finds it difficult to settle in one place. He smiles with bittersweet amusement when he explains that, at his age, it is time he found a permanent place of residence, and sat down to write his novel about Africa, *Land of Fire*. He came to Ibiza, he says, on the trail of a young woman. Now he lives alone, with occasional happy visits from his partner, at Can Embarcador.

An unexpectedly relaxed atmosphere prevails throughout the various rooms of this house, in keeping with the spirit of those who live there.

The House of the Virgins

On the highway that leads from the capital of Ibiza to the coves on the north side of the island, a blue-painted stone marks a road that snakes through pine forests; it ends at a house that, being a combination of a modern addition built onto the side of a small rural dwelling, has unusually elongated proportions. This is where Jörg Marquard lives, one of several interior designers whose work has made a major impact on the old houses in Ibiza that have been restored and modernized.

Jörg Marquard is a friendly, serious person who is keen to establish a relationship of mutual understanding with his clients concerning the common objective of producing comfortable living spaces. His all-embracing philosophy is simple, empirical, and very open to understanding human nature.

Living for many years in Ibiza has on the one hand stimulated and honed his creative drive, and on the other produced in him a certain measured detachment from many things that are happening in the wider world. Perhaps for him his house is a space where normality reigns, where nothing is discordant. To the comfortable rural structure of

filled with objects, brimming with shapes and colors, there is a common and unusual point of reference: a seemingly infinite number of sculptures, a veritable army of hieratic upright forms, which on closer inspection reveal delicately facial features and hands. They crowd every shelf and table, and any level surface.

The strangely schematized shapes of the bodies immediately suggests marionettes, puppets, or mannequins, however, the indescribably beatific expressions of the faces are the real clue: they are folk carvings of the Virgin Mary, which Jörg Marquard has collected over many years but whose motley and rather gaudy clothes he has removed. As the result of this brutal gesture of reductionism the figures have taken on the uniform and ambiguous appearance that has made of them interesting works of art. What comes to mind is one of Ingmar Bergman's late films: it might be *Fanny and Alexander*, in which children stand dumbfounded at the

the preexisting building he has added new living spaces and bedrooms, as well as a working area, which form an access courtyard in the north side of the building. The south side of the house, set with porches that are filled with books and plants, looks onto the valley, with the garden laid out around the swimming pool and an outdoor dining area. The comfortable, relaxed atmosphere that pervades the house is echoed by the easygoing lifestyle of the inhabitants, most volubly two blond-haired children who mimic Michael Jordan as they play at basketball or go crashing into the swimming pool.

Though no part of the design makes an explicit statement, and without it being necessary to proclaim the fact, this house possesses an indefinable Ibizan style in the way it is lit, in its naturalness, in its mixture of references to parallel cultures, from prints by Piranesi, which underscore the atmosphere of an art gallery to the furniture painted by Jörg Marquard, most notably the beds, which is reminiscent of the products of Roger Fry's Omega Workshops. There reigns a natural and controlled disorder or, put another way, a free and spontaneous order. In all these rooms, that are

In this interior scheme full of warmth and heirlooms, the presence of hundreds of unclothed Virgins creates an atmosphere that is both peaceful and disturbing.

door of their uncle's doll workshop. To live in such a house is to meet, several hundred times in day, the gaze of a pair of blue eyes that exude goodwill and understanding. Sometimes those understanding blue eyes seem to burn with irrepressible life; they are the eyes of the woman who lives in the house, ruling it with the sure hand of a ship's captain.

Arcades, a swimming pool, and a summer
dining room make for a comfortable lifestyle
and are well suited to the climate.

Can Marés

From the city of Ibiza the road to Jesús, a little village that has been absorbed by the capital and that is notable for the impressive painted altarpiece of its church, leads to a place where the land rises steeply; turn around and you will be rewarded by one of the best views of medieval Dalt Vila and the port. The slopes facing Levante lead to the yellowish fairways of the island's only golf course; if you continue northward, however, you will come upon the network of small narrow roads that traverse the area known as Can Furnet. A dense stand of pine trees comes into view on the sharp corners of the narrow road that leads up to a small hill. The wood stands in a silence is broken only by the thrum of cicadas and the infrequent whispering of the wind from Levante. At the top of the hill rises an elegant white house that offers the cubelike outline of its building in the north-facing façade and opens its generously proportioned porch onto the lawn in front of the swimming pool. The pool descends southward in tiered terraces, and through the warm mist one can make out the outline of Formentera.

The house was built by Rolph Blakstad and has had all the benefit of his discriminating eclecticism: while some rooms are authentically "Ibizan", others have drawn from quite different sources of inspiration. The entrance hall, an unusual irregular space with a great wooden staircase, rises grandly through two stories and is hung with gigantic reproduction Renaissance portraits – women painted in profile. The sitting room uncompromisingly evokes grand old Mediterranean houses, with four tall molded pillars that emphasize the great feeling of space.

The rest of the house comprises a sequence of rooms with a succession of chimney pieces, carved staircases set against white walls, arcades and wooden pergolas. Here, in the play of dark and light tones and crisp white outlines, is the ageless formula of Mediterranean architecture.

The hallway, irregular in shape and with a staircase leading up to the bedrooms, is transformed into a room in its own right by a collection of beautiful large-scale paintings.

Do-Doce

One of the most beautiful routes that the ever more invasive traffic follows along the network of Ibizan roads is the straight road that runs from the capital up to San Rafael. The magical silhouette of the village church stands as a permanent landmark, while the changing light illuminates the different angles of its belfry.

Just before the village a smaller road branches off this route, cutting through an area typical of the island's nightlife, and disappears into a dense stand of pine and oak. This road leads up toward the Serreta de Can Palau, a pocket of almost virgin land between the great mountain of Sa Murta and the San Antonio road.

Many years ago, a German businessman purchased the 18th-century Ibizan house which now bears the name of his first wife, Do, to which he added "Doce" (twelve), the number of rooms that the owner has fitted out for his large family. The property is in fact nothing less than a small hamlet, the result of adding extensions to old buildings; the most recent of those extensions contains a suite of staggered guest rooms that form a convenient angle with the two-storey porch.

The fragmented nature of the house – the multiplicity of its component parts in a sort of Ibizan collage – means that it has none of the purism of the island's newly-built houses, but it also gives it that indefinable style that, so it is supposed, is preferred by a certain social class in Ibiza.

The land attached to the house, cut into ancient agricultural terraces whose origin some historians have attributed to the Phoenicians, has been altered. The land has become an extensive garden bisected by cascades of water that at every fall spills into small tanks; this is the "natural" landscape in which stands the house.

From the uppermost terrace, beneath red bougainvillaea, can be felt the cool south wind that blows from the mysterious rock of Es Vedrà. Despite all its contradictions, this heavenly spot is surely much more desirable than the broken outline of San Antonio Bay that can be made out toward Poniente.

A lone light is still shining in the house: it comes from a small studio where the owner's wife is at work, her nimble hands making small items of gold jewelry.

Previous pages: the master bedroom and bathroom, in the oldest part of the house. Certain elements that have been added in the style of a collage add a vertical dimension to the old rooms.

One of the most atmospheric of the renovated rooms is the old kitchen, now converted into the sitting room, which leads through to a small studio on another level.